W9-CMM-721

Faithfully Yours

Earle V. Pierce

FIRST BAPTIST CHURCH
16TH & "O" STS., N. W.
WASHINGTON 6, D. C.

322
PIE

THE CHURCH AND WORLD CONDITIONS

By
EARLE V. PIERCE, D.D.
Author of " The Conflict Within My Self "
With an Introduction by
KENNETH S. LATOURETTE, D.D., Ph.D.

Published by
The Blakiston Company
PHILADELPHIA

Distributed by
Fleming H. Revell Company
NEW YORK AND LONDON

Copyright, MCMXLIII, by
FLEMING H. REVELL COMPANY

*This book has been manufactured in this form
in compliance with orders of the War Production
Board for the conservation of paper and other materials necessary for the prosecution of the War.*

Printed in the United States of America

New York: 158 Fifth Avenue
London: 99 Anerley Road

To
The Memory of
My Parents
Who
By Example and Precept
Taught me to Reverence and Love the Church

INTRODUCTION

IT is a pleasure and an honor to be requested to write a brief introduction to this little book. Dr. Pierce's well known concern for the loyalty of the Church to our Lord and for the world-wide spread of the Gospel here find eloquent and impassioned expression.

The emphasis of the book, as is proper, is in its culminating chapter. Dr. Pierce believes that in spite of its past failures and the present weaknesses which come from the sins and the lack of full commitment to Christ of its members, "the Church can still mightily improve conditions in the world." He is convinced that the power of God is freely available to those who fulfill the conditions of repentance, faith, and obedience, and that, equipped with this power, the Church can do much to remedy the present tragic plight of mankind. He stresses the obligation greatly to enlarge the missionary enterprise.

As a colleague of Dr. Pierce on the Board of Managers of the American Baptist Foreign Mission Society, I am particularly glad of this emphasis. The urgent need of the world is for an augmented Christian missionary effort of the Church. This must not be primarily in numbers, although added personnel is needed. It must be in a quality of life. We must have more of those who unmistakably are bearing what Paul calls "the fruit of the Spirit"—"love, joy, peace, long-suffering, gentleness, goodness, faith, meekness, self-control." Missionaries of this description can come only from a Church which is overflowing with this kind of life. Our prayer must be, to use the words of a great Chinese Christian: "Lord, revive Thy Church, beginning with me."

It is a ground for hope in these stormy days that here and there, in many countries and among many branches of Christ's Church, there are those who are praying in this fashion. Groups, many of them small, and individuals, often in the midst of great tribulation, are giving evidence of that strength which is " made perfect in weekness." Any of us may join this company. It is through such as these that God is working and will continue to work.

KENNETH S. LATOURETTE.

Yale University.

FOREWORD

From earliest infancy I was taken in my mother's arms to the service of worship in the church and elsewhere, and thus, according to the findings of modern psychologists, my infant mind was pre-empted by spiritual influences that have ever inclined me toward the Church.

From childhood on I was in the Sunday school, and went with my parents to special evangelistic services, although this meant an hour's drive with the farm team. It would be two in the afternoon before we were home from church, having taken off the edge a little from a vigorous appetite by the cookies which had been taken along. Returning from evangelistic services at night, it was always late, but my parents wanted their four children to have the best, and that meant the things of God.

Family worship was the rule. Preachers and church workers were often at our home. Sunday was a holy and a happy day. There was a sacred and beautiful serenity about it. Afternoon Sunday school at the country schoolhouse was the usual thing, and my father much of the time the leader of it. Frequently after this, on fine days, was a family walk down into the woods and to the lake. Deep emotions stir me as I think of what a Christian Sabbath and a Christian home were in those days. The Church, the Bible, the Worship, and Christians were all something holy, and made us conscious of the eternal world. The ideals of life were shaped from above.

When the *Gospel Songs* first came out, the people of the neighborhood, Christians and others, used to gather at a home Sunday nights and spend the whole evening singing these songs. No movies, taverns, worldly broadcasts, or

7

night clubs then threw their baleful darkness over the souls of youth. From the Sabbath we went into the week refreshed.

It is such communities as my parents and grandparents before them helped to make that account for the best in America, and it is with a homesickness for those days and prayer that the vital elements of the fear of God and the love and respect for the things of His Kingdom that I have undertaken to write this book, calling, as well as I can, to the pastors and the Church to " seek the Lord while he may be found; to call upon him while he is near," and beseeching that the wicked forsake their way and the unrighteous men their thoughts and that they return unto the Lord, who will have mercy upon them and to our God, for He will abundantly pardon.

The Church alone can show the way to a " just and durable peace," but it can do so only if the Church herself shall see her failure and repent and turn to God. The passage just quoted from Isaiah was spoken not to the pagan world but to God's people, and it ought to thunder in our ears today, that we may return to the God of our fathers.

The substance of these chapters has been given as addresses for the past two years in various parts of the country, before churches, conventions and schools, and God has so used them to help so many people that I have heeded the frequent request that they be put into printed form, with the hope of a wider usefulness.

I am greatly indebted to Dr. William B. Lipphard, editor of *Missions;* to Dr. Jesse R. Wilson, home secretary of the American Baptist Foreign Mission Society; Dr. R. Wilbur Babcock, of Temple Baptist Church, Minneapolis; Dr. W. B. Riley, president of the Northwestern Evangelical Seminary, Minneapolis; Dr. J. C. Robbins, president of the Northern Baptist Convention, and Prof. Kenneth S. Latourette of Yale

University, for careful reading of the manuscript and many valuable suggestions, and for their warm encouragement that I put forth the book. I wish also to acknowledge definite help which has come to me from writers whom I have quoted literally or in substance.

If God shall use this in any degree to help forward the basic revival of spiritual values in America and the world, this shall be my full compensation for the time spent in the preparation. I am keenly aware of its inadequacy, but " who is sufficient for these things? " God, who so often uses " the weak things to confound the mighty," may use this to His glory.

E. V. P.

Minneapolis, Minn.

CONTENTS

I

THE CRISIS UPON US

The Pharisees also with the Sadducees came, and tempting desired him that he would shew them a sign from heaven.

He answered and said unto them, When it is evening, ye say, It will be fair weather: for the sky is red.

And in the morning, It will be foul weather to day: for the sky is red and lowring. O ye hypocrites, ye can discern the face of the sky; but can ye not discern the signs of the times?
—MATT. 16: 1-3.

ARE we awake to the tragic significance of the days in which we are living and in which multitudes are violently dying? Is the Church in danger of falling under our Lord's indictment in that, while we can forecast the weather far more accurately than the ancients could, we are as dull of apprehension, as stupid, as wilfully ignorant concerning the meaning of this storm which has burst with such fury upon our heads as were those of old?

Our Lord sternly condemned Israel, and their religious leaders, because they were so blind to plain indications of the tragedy of the times in which they were living. They had no eyes for the Messiah who came in different guise from that which they were expecting. They had no sensitiveness to the sins that were eating the heart out of the nation and making it ripe for destruction. They were smug and complacent in the presence of a dry and sterile intellectual monotheism, and were lacking in the life and the spirit of the God whom they thought they worshiped.

God had judged Israel many times for their sins and had

13

punished the nation severely. At Kadesh-barnea a whole generation was doomed to death in the wilderness, because they did not have faith in God to go in and possess the land. Arriving in Canaan, victories attended their obedience, defeats and enslavement their disobedience. Revivals were sent again and again: these would bless them for a time and then they would backslide into idolatry and sensual sin. The northern kingdom was swept into permanent dissolution. Later the southern kingdom went into the seventy years' captivity, because they did not see or understand. Prophet after prophet sought to open their eyes and lead them into the ways of God, but still they sinned and sank into carnality.

Now for four hundred years God had let them go on with only priestly leadership, no great prophet arising, until John the Baptist came announcing that the Messiah was at hand. But the heralded King was not of their kind, not even what John had expected Him to be. He neither drove out the Roman rule, nor did he take the ax and start at once chopping down the fruitless tree. But had the leaders of Israel known truly their past, they would have feared for their future. In the miracles of Jesus they beheld the power of God. In the messages of Jesus they saw His standards of righteousness which convicted them of sin. In His typical acts of judgment, the cleansing of the temple, the cursing of the barren fig tree, the command to the demons to enter into the swine, they saw how His power might be used.

The crucial time with that generation is pictured in the twelfth chapter of Matthew where, after all the compassion, beneficent deeds, and wondrous words of Jesus, the Pharisees charged Him with being in league with Satan. He warned them against this attitude, this failure to discern between the Holy Spirit and the devil, its danger being that it would become eternal and thus of necessity be unforgivable. Here is the nadir of fruitlessness, spiritual rottenness instead of ripeness, perverseness utterly pernicious. From that time on He sought no more to save the rulers, the Pharisees, the scribes, the Sadducees. He quoted Isaiah's indictment as especially timely. " This people's heart is waxed gross, and their ears are dull of hearing, and their eyes they have closed." Three steps are here marked in a fatal descent. First, the carnal evaluation of life, the " heart waxed gross," dulled their soul's ear to the voice of God; then sheer perversity, the wilful closing of their eyes to the revelation of God which was being made, sealed their doom. They had stoned and killed the prophets who had been sent unto them —the earlier servants sent to gather the fruit; now they are about to kill the Son and cast Him out of the vineyard. The end of the Jewish dispensation is at hand. That which was begun by Moses, who molded them into a nation and led them to the Promised Land, is shortly to come to an end. The people who had been so carefully gathered and separated from the nations are now to be scattered among them. They could tell what the weather of the next day was going to be, but they could not sense the storm that was to strike out of heaven upon them. The call of John the Baptist to repent had gone unheeded by the rulers. The call which Jesus took up, " Repent ye, for the kingdom of heaven is at hand," was alike unheeded. They will not repent; they must be punished, and the way made for " a nation bringing forth the fruit."

The Church and the Signs of the Times

The Christian era had a beginning. It will have an end. Its beginning and continuance was a " mystery " hid from the prophets who foretold the Messianic Kingdom. They thought that, with the coming of the Messiah, His Kingdom should be set up on the earth in glorious power. They did not see the long interval between His first and second comings which was to be filled in by His Church. Is the Church to be as undiscerning as was Israel to its tragic end?

When the Church period was about to open, Christ did forecast (as recorded in the thirteenth chapter of Matthew, and in other places) the course and the end of the work of His Kingdom of gospel and grace which should be carried forward by the Church. In parable, as He was entering into Jerusalem, He described Himself as the nobleman who was going away into a far country " to receive for himself the kingdom," that is, in its glorious power and manifestation, " and to return." He described elsewhere accurately enough for anyone to know the conditions which should prevail at the time of His return—the tares grown up among the wheat, the slothful and drunken servants, the failure to be watchful for the work which he had assigned to His servants, and the near eclipse of " the faith," saying, " But when the Son of man cometh shall he find the faith on the earth? " The logical answer from the context is no. Relatively it would have disappeared. If the letter to the church at Laodicea is typical of the last period of the Christian Church, then there is exhibited outward magnificence, smug self-satisfaction, poverty of spirit, blindness of spiritual perception, dullness of hearing.

We need not be concerned about the multitude of minor " signs of the times," which many make so much of, but which can be found to have been in abundance in every century of Christian history; but there are certain great and mighty movements today, discerned by a few, that should cause us to pause and to say seriously, " What next? "

What is the meaning of this present crisis? The prophets of old saw in famine and pestilence and the devastation of defeat in battle the judgment of God upon the nation because of their sins. The prophets were God-conscious, as well as man-conscious. They believed in the imminence of God, as well as in His transcendence. We say, "*It* thunders; *it* rains," making nature an impersonal thing. They said, with a discernment that modern science is today dimly approaching, "Jehovah thundereth"; "Thou waterest the earth." They saw that the Creator was not "cribbed, cabined, and confined" in the universe which He had made, but was the One "who covereth thyself with light as with a garment . . . who maketh the clouds his chariot; who walketh upon the wings of the wind." He was mindful of His people and was a Shepherd leading them forth when they obeyed Him, but He punished them when they disobeyed.

Granted that, during the kindergarten period of religion, which was the Jewish, God adapted Himself to Israel quite definitely, as you have to do with a child, with rewards and punishments, still He is the same God; and although the Christian Church was sent forth "as sheep among wolves," and Jesus said definitely, "In the world ye shall have tribulation," we cannot believe for a moment that among the great nations of the west, wherein the Gospel has had the chance to become so dominant, God would have permitted such devastating wrath to break forth, had there not been long and perverse and inexcusable sin and neglect of His Word and work. If you take the view that judgment comes only as a natural sequence to the violation of holy law, even so it is time to look carefully and see what holy laws have been violated to precipitate such ghastly devastation on earth.

"What Meaneth This?"

Certainly we are in days unprecedented. Never before has the whole earth been involved in such a war—so inexcusable, so colossal, so universal, so devilish, so destructive. What are men saying about it?

It is significant that students of prophecy, not wild fanatics, but careful, intelligent students of the Word of God, are believing with wonderful unanimity that we are actually approaching the end of the Christian era, and that the coming of Christ cannot be far away, as we count years. Added to this is the testimony of great theologians like Adolph Keller of Switzerland. Following the great ecumenical conferences of Oxford and Edinburgh in 1937, he wrote his tremendous book, small in size, but terrific in force, *Five Minutes to Twelve*. On the front cover is the picture of a clock with the hour hand at twelve, and the minute hand at eleven—five minutes to twelve; and his thesis is that we are that close to the major crisis of history. "We had forgotten," he says, " that the Bible does NOT speak of a world which grows better and better day by day, in an eternal process of evolution, but rather of a Judgment Day which would bring the world to an end. We took our civilization for granted and did not listen to the ominous trampling of the hoofs of the apocalyptic steeds which caused the earth to tremble in fear and in despair." And as to the causes which are working, he declares:

"Things happen which could hardly have been planned by men; they bear the mark of a sinister and demonic intelligence, of Satanic cunning. . . . A dark and demonic world has made an incursion into human life. And these powers seem to pursue hidden aims and ends, to manifest themselves willfully and emotionally, and so palpably to annul the shape and image of personal tendencies and beings that it is difficult not to believe the Bible when it speaks of the prince of this world and the sinister host of principalities and powers with which we have got to battle." *

But others than theologians are saying strange things. A friend of mine was in a meeting of some two hundred big

* *Five Minutes to Twelve,* by Adolph Keller, Cokesbury Press, pp. 29ff.

business men in the fall of 1940, called together by a large manufacturer whom he knew, who presided. His first sentence in opening the meeting was, " Gentlemen, I am not a religious man; but I believe that Jesus Christ is coming back to this world very soon. And my reason for believing this is because He is the only one that can possibly get us out of this awful mess that we are in." H. G. Wells some time ago said, " Civilization is a constant race between education and chaos." Later he said, " Civilization is not slipping into chaos; it is already there." President George Maynard Hutchins of the University of Chicago said in an address recently:

" Victory cannot save civilization. It can merely prevent its destruction by one spectacular method. Since civilization was well on its way to destruction before the war began, success in the war will not automatically preserve it. The domination of the world by England, the United States, and Russia is not identical with civilization. The victory of these powers gives mankind a better chance to be civilized than their defeat. Whether or not mankind will take that chance depends on the kind of intellectual, moral and spiritual leadership it has."

Nehru, of India, who with his father and Gandhi have given England much trouble in their effort to secure nationalism for India, wrote his autobiography during the first seven of his imprisonments. He has no religion, having turned aside even from Hinduism. He says, " We are unquestionably at the end of an era, and no one can tell what the next is to be." Professor Sorokin of Harvard declares in *The Crisis of Our Age* that for the past four hundred years the Western world has been descending from a civilization spiritually centered to one now wholly sensate in which everything is judged by the senses, and that we have now arrived at a stage of utter rottenness, reflected in art, music, literature, law and morals.

Former Blindness

World conditions today are alarming to the last degree. Before World War I we were smiling with comfortable complacency that the world would learn war no more, that it was already beating its swords into plowshares and its spears into pruning hooks. We were confident that labor would never permit another great armed strife; and, on the other hand, that the financiers would never furnish the money for it. And, beyond all this, our culture was so great that it would not permit our stooping to the degradation of such a slaughter.

Germany had no such civilized illusions. It was confidently looking forward to *Der Tag,* when it could put the other nations into their proper places and get for itself its place in the sun. By pressure from Russia, the Archduke Ferdinand was assassinated in Serbia. This was the spark which touched off the powder keg. Germany declared *Der Tag* had arrived; and this most cultured nation revealed that her culture was *kultur*, a determination to dominate at all cost and with any means, even to poison gas, the nations of the world.

After four unspeakably horrible years for all the world, the movement which she started with such furious confidence was stopped. A peace was forced upon the foe, but it was a peace that by its very nature could not be permanent. It was but a sowing of the dragon's teeth. Germany tried to stagger along as a republic, but for this she had no preparation in her former government or culture and now she received no help, idealistically or materially, from France, England, or America, except that Mr. Dawes consented to go to Germany and help to establish a stable financial system. It is commonly thought or rather known that Hitler's rise was partially encouraged by some French and British interests, which, like the German interests, saw in Hitler protection for themselves against communism.

Then the revolution in Russia broke forth. Not only royalty were ruthlessly slain, but millions of Christian peasants were put to death. Antichrist was now in power. Communism sprang up as one of the swiftest, mightiest, and most ruthless movements which the world has ever known. Italy blocked it with the fascism which Mussolini introduced. Under the fearful crushing force of poverty, dismembered states, bankruptcy, and the rise of crime, the soil was ripe in Germany for the germination, growth, and fructification of a thistle seed of most virulent power by the name of Adolph Hitler. His book, *Mein Kampf*, had informed the world what this movement was to be. It was not anything done in a corner, but openly, and we have seen the swift rise of the Nazi power based on an ideology that has swept Germany, even as communism swept Russia. But it has been scarcely less antichrist in its ideas and execution. It arose to subdue everything else and to make for itself not only a place in the sun with the rest of the nations, but to make itself the veritable Sun, with all other nations only enslaved planets revolving in orbits which it might prescribe.

In all this came the opportunity for Shintoism to come into fearful flowering and awful fruitage, a religion and a state essentially one, claiming to be supreme because the state was declared to be God-born. Antichrist has arisen in Japan to throttle the Orient at least.

Our missionaries who have been long in Japan tell us that, following the Conference on Naval Limitation in which the 5-5-3 ratio among Great Britain, the United States, and Japan was determined upon, the Japanese army was reduced by 50,000. This threw many an officer out of a job. These officers were astute enough to ask for places in the schools. These were given to them, and the militarists were thus scattered through the schools of Japan. They began systematically the cultivation of the militaristic idea which we have now seen come to its full stature. Within fifteen years they were able to make a demonstration before the emperor that laid the foundation for and gave confidence for the aggression which has now been launched.

Italy not only determined to adopt fascism, but she became drunk with lust for the power and grandeur of the ancient empire, and prepared to take her place in asserting her supremacy over other nations.

Therefore, there has come about that coalescence of evil forces in the world, that birth of a trinity of Satanic nationalities, that conjunction of three evil stars of first magnitude, to make a burning sun to blight and blast the earth; and that blighting and blasting are going on with demoniacal power. Never before has the whole earth been armed to the teeth as it is today. Xerxes indeed amassed an army of a million, but it did not last long. Napoleon in his vast conquest never had more than 750,000 men in arms at once. In the War Between the States upwards of four million men were in arms. In the First World War ten million soldiers were in the conflict at one time. But today, with almost every nation lined up for the Axis powers or against them, there are fifty million or more men in fighting or in training, and all of the vast achievements in material inventions are being turned to the work of fearful and unprecedented destruction.

Whose Is the Blame?

Now, the question arises, Whence came all this? Who is responsible? Are only the aggressor nations to be charged with this evil? Is it just something which devils and wicked men have hatched up, thinking they could now carry through their program of enslavement? Or can it be that the Christian Church, which is suffering so much on her mission fields and at home, is in some way linked up with a definite and inescapable responsibility for all of this? Were the prophets of old right who thought religiously upon national questions? Is this God's judgment upon His people for not having served Him as they ought? God has not changed. He still has His people in the world. They have a mission and a message and a power. They have been sent to do something. Can it be that God is again visiting judgment upon humanity because His Christian people have failed in their work of serving Him? Is He using nations, as of old, to be the whips of His chastisements? Has the Church failed to use power given to it to prevent the world becoming such a slaughterhouse? Is there " sin in the camp " as of old, covetousness, disobedience, spiritual stupidity, that has precipitated all this?

This question must be frankly faced. Israel was finally broken and scattered to the four winds of heaven because she had so tragically failed in the task set before her. God does not love the Christian Church any more than He loved Israel, and He will reckon with her just as certainly. We must not hesitate to face hard facts. Dr. Henry Van Dyke declared that it was " better to believe the saddest truth than the merriest lie." In the past we have believed very many merry lies, and have paid well for this false faith. Here we are being blown into chaos, and no one can tell what the end will be. I propose to examine this question of the place of the Church in the world and of its responsibility for the present condition and the possibility of its still having a deciding influence in the destiny of the world. Men are talking comfortably and bravely about establishing a " just and durable peace." But with what? " The work of righteousness shall be peace, and the effect of righteousness quietness and assurance forever," declared the inspired prophet, speaking for God. Can there be a " just and durable peace " with nine-tenths of the men of the world yet in their sins? Will you build a staunch international ship of state out of the rotten timbers of unregenerate humanity? The Christian Church must awake to her God-given power and province, to the miracle work of remaking men in vast numbers, and that swiftly, into the life and spirit of the Lord, or all reconstruction will but end in further and more terrible destruction. Professor Sorokin closes his great work with the appeal:

" The more unteachable we are, and the less freely and willingly we choose the sole course of salvation open to us, the more inexorable will be the coercion, the more pitiless the ordeal, the more terrible the *dies irae* of the transition. Let us hope that the grace of understanding may be vouchsafed us and that we may choose, before it is too late, the right road—the road that leads not to death but to the further realization of man's unique creative mission on this planet! " *

Let us indeed " hope " and " choose " as we ought, but we will find that all hope is in vain which is not in an awakened Christianity, and that the " right road " is that of " repentance toward God and faith in the Lord Jesus Christ " pointed out by the great apostle to the Gentiles at the beginning of the Christian era.

* *The Crisis of Our Age,* Dutton, p. 326.

II

THE PURPOSE, PROGRAM AND POWER OF THE CHRISTIAN CHURCH

But ye shall receive power, after that the Holy Spirit is come upon you: and ye shall be witnesses unto me both in Jerusalem, and in all Judæa and Samaria, and unto the uttermost part of the earth.—ACTS 1: 8.

OUR first proposition is that the Christian Church was launched with a purpose, a program, and a power sufficient, had it remained pure, to have so changed world conditions that the cataclysm we are now suffering would never have needed to come.

I. THE PURPOSE OF THE CHURCH

The purpose of the Church is plainly stated in two passages of Scripture. In John 3: 17 we read, " For God sent not his son into the world to condemn the world [that is, the first time that He came] but that the world through him might be saved." And in John 20: 21, after Christ's resurrection, when He appeared to the disciples, He made the astounding statement, the greatest utterance which He ever made concerning the Church, " As the Father sent me, even so send I you."

Nothing could be plainer. The Father sent Him most certainly to save the world. He wrought out the necessary redemption for man's sin. He brought forth the glorious Gospel of the love of God and His willingness to forgive men on the basis of the sacrifice which He had made; and now

He commissions the Church to go forward and complete the salvation of the world through the power of the Gospel which He had given, and through that of the Holy Spirit.

Objections Appear

Immediately when this statement is made that the Church was sent to save the world objections are raised. The first is that the Church was not sent to save the world, but to save people out of the world; that the world is a hopeless wreck and it is useless to try to save it; that God Himself has given it over to destruction, and that all the Church can do is to gather as many as possible out of the world and save them unto a life eternal.

It is true that the Church is sent to save people out of the world. It is true also that the Church is sent to save the world. Both statements are true when rightly understood.

One great part of the program of the Church is to improve the conditions of society in order that a larger number of people may be saved out of the world. It certainly should be obvious to anyone that there are at times certain sweeping social conditions that make it almost impossible to save anyone, and only as evil is curbed on a gigantic scale can we reach the individuals to save them. Lecky tells us that the revivals of the Wesleys saved England from a vast and horrible industrial and political revolution, such as France suffered; and by doing this the Wesleys made it possible to save hundreds of thousands who otherwise could not have been saved. What chance was there for evangelism during the French Revolution or even for a long time after? What could missionaries have done there? Very little. The apostle Paul tells us to " pray for kings and all that are in authority, that we may live a quiet and godly life." It is in times of peace and quiet that the Gospel makes its great gains. It was under the peace which the Roman Empire succeeded in imposing upon the world that the Gospel first had its opportunity of spreading with almost lightning-like rapidity. Can anyone say that in America we are now having the opportunity to save youth that we had during prohibition days? They are being swept on to destruction by this great flood of alcohol, which was ushered in at first unconstitutionally by permitting the sale of 3.2 per cent beer before prohibition was repealed, and which then rose to a flood tide by repeal. Alcohol has been scientifically defined as " the most deadly of all slow poisons," and from its physical, mental, social and spiritual effects might well be renamed alcohell. Repeal was carried through because of the supineness of the Christian Church. Less than twenty-five per cent of the electorate voted for repeal. It could have been defeated, as it was in South Carolina, by an aroused church, and thus we could still be having sober conditions in which to save men and women.

The Federal Council of Churches has given an illuminating study of the effect of war upon evangelism. It has shown by a mathematically accurate graph that during times of war, evangelism, instead of rising, suffers a sudden and notable decline. If more souls are saved during this war than in peace times, it will be a marked exception and will be because God's people shall have become humble to a point where God can give a revival.

No, the Christian Church had as one great task, because it had the power, to change social and political conditions so that the fullest possible quota of individuals might be saved " out of the world." Dr. W. Graham Scroggie, who certainly believes as strongly as anyone in the second coming of Christ and in related truths, says in his comment upon the revival wrought through the king, Josiah:

" There are many good people who, because the Bible predicts that the world shall get worse and worse, think it is no business of theirs to attempt to arrest the evil. Such a view as that leads to moral paralysis. Josiah knew that he could not save that nation from speedy ruin; but he, at least, would postpone the inevitable and make it more difficult for them to go to their doom. To that task also we are called, for history is repeating itself. We may not be able to save civilization, but certainly we are not to sit with folded arms and watch it topple into the abyss. Let the church renew the covenant. The Law preceded the Gospel and ever must."

The Predicted Apostasy

Other objectors say, " It is predicted that evil men shall wax worse and worse and that even the Church shall turn apostate, so that when the Son of Man comes, He will find but little of the faith upon the earth." Yes, this is surely predicted. But those who rest in this, as the reason for their undertaking nothing in the line of establishing social and political righteousness in the earth, forget that *predictions are not compelling;* they are only revealing. They are pre-written history and not premolded history. As proof of this, I cite both Jeremiah and Jesus.

Jeremiah is about the bravest man to be found in all the Bible, for he carried himself throughout life most courageously under the hardest lifelong task that was ever assigned to anyone. He was called as a youth to be a prophet of God to the people Israel, and was told that his message to them should be that, if they did not repent of their sins and turn to God, He would send them into captivity. If they would repent, then the captivity need not come; but if they did not repent, it would have to come. And God told him plainly, in addition, that the people *would not repent.* God predicted the unrepentant spirit and He predicted the captivity, and yet He said that neither was necessary; and He sent His prophet for a lifetime to convey His message of yearning love and to urge the people to return unto Him.

Jeremiah took this commission. During the first part of his life he carried it out with much inner resistance. He even said that he made up his mind he would hold his peace and not say anything, but he found he could not do that; for the fire burned within him and he had to speak out. During the latter part of his life, he accepted the situation and never complained again, but went forward with the people, warning them, pleading with them, and finally suffering captivity with them, as they refused to repent.

Our Lord plainly predicted the destruction of Jerusalem and the scattering of the people, and yet at the end of His ministry He wept over Jerusalem, saying, " If thou hadst known, even thou, at least in this thy day, the things that belong unto thy peace; but now they are hid from thine eyes . . . I would have gathered thy children together, even as a hen gathers her chickens under her wings, but ye would not! Behold, your house is left unto you desolate." Christ predicted the destruction of Jerusalem, but He said it need not have been destroyed.

Therefore, we are not to let the predictions in the Bible of the corruption which would accumulate in the world and of the destruction which would come upon an apostate Church and upon the world deter us from carrying forward a program for salvation of men and for the salvation of society in order that more men may be saved. Nor can we let this excuse us from our responsibility or from the Church's responsibility for the world being in the awful mess that it is now in. Nor from future responsibility. We do not know when Christ is coming—it may be centuries ahead. We must be at our *entire* work, individual and social.

A World Defeated by Christ

Let us remember also that the Lord never launched His Church upon its program of mediating His redemption to a lost world until He could say, " Be of good cheer, I have overcome the world." This was no idly optimistic statement. It was a defeated world into which He sent His Church. He had won the crucial battle and had been able to say, " I saw Satan fall like lightning from heaven." The Church was but to follow up the victory which He had already accomplished, and it has not done so. Following the battle of Gettysburg, in which Lee's army was defeated, scattered, and started upon its disastrous retreat, General Meade, who had wrought the victory for the north, rested upon his laurels, and let Lee escape. When Lincoln heard of this, he was furious. He saw the vast mistake which Meade had made. He saw that, had Meade immediately followed up his victory, he could have crushed Lee's army a long way from its base of supplies and before it had had a chance to reinforce or reorganize itself, and that Meade perhaps could have brought the terrible war to an end then and there. Lincoln was so sure of this, and so certain of the mistake which Meade had made, that for a time he thought seriously of disciplining him. But then his generous nature asserted itself, and he said, " No, a great victory has been won. We will not cloud it with any disciplining of the general who has wrought the victory." But the decision of history has been that Meade was grossly culpable in that he did not follow up his initial victory with a complete one. Lee would have done so, great soldier that he was. The Church has made a similar mistake. It has not finished the victory our Lord so gloriously began, as it might have done. It has not conquered as it could have. The purpose of the Church was to put down evil which was ruining mankind as it had power and to save men while it was doing this, and because it was doing it.

II. POWER WAS GIVEN TO THE CHURCH

The power which was given to the Church was sufficient

for the purpose. When our Lord said to His disciples, " Ye shall receive power, after that the Holy Spirit is come upon you," He said a most tremendous thing. " Power belongeth unto God," declared the prophet of old; and power, then, is a manifestation of God. The power of the Holy Spirit is certainly the power of God. His is the power which created this universe and flung it out into space. His is the power which created man in the image of God, and is the power able to recreate him. Christ's statement means in the context that *the Church has the ability to do all that the Church was sent to do.* It means sufficiency for the task. The Church is a group of disciples endued with power. To speak of a weak Church is thus a contradiction of terms. The Lord equipped His people for His work. The Church, in His mind, *is power.*

It was, first of all, not political power, as the disciples wanted, but spiritual; though later it was to include political power as God's people had that power placed in their hands for right government of the state of which they would become a dominant part.

Christ's Power Ours

The Church's power was the same as that which had equipped the Son of God for His earthly work, by which He had " overcome the world." A careful study of the gospels reveals that Jesus never did anything that God could not empower a man to do. The incarnation was absolute. It was the Son of God's self-limitation to the condition of humanity. He utterly became man at the same time He remained the Son of God. He came upon earth to live as a man, to enter our humanity, to work as a man, under His Heavenly Father. He makes that very plain: " I can of myself do nothing; as I hear I judge: and my judgment is just; because I seek not mine own will but the will of him that sent me " (John 5: 30). And again, " I speak to the world those things which I have heard of him " (John 8: 26). And again, " Verily, verily, I say unto you, the Son can do nothing of himself, but what he seeth the Father do " (John 5: 19). The gospel of John, which exalts the deity of our Lord, also magnifies the fact that the " Word became flesh." It is the gospel of the perfect incarnation of the eternal Son of God.

We must not be so afraid of losing sight of the glory of the utter and essential deity of Jesus that we fail to see the glory of His utter and essential humanity while He was here upon earth. He shows to us what was possible to one wholly surrendered unto God the Father. Can you think of anything that Jesus ever did that God did not enable men also through the Holy Spirit to do? In fact, Jesus said, " He that believeth on me the works that I do shall he do also, and greater works than these shall he do; because I go unto the Father.' Jesus spoke truth from God, and so did the apostles after the Day of Pentecost. Jesus healed men, and so did the apostles, through the power of God. Jesus had victory over temptation, and so did men, through the power of God. Jesus raised people from the dead, and so did the apostles, through the power of the same Holy Spirit. Jesus died a crucial death of sacrificial love upon the cross and rose again from the dead. He told His disciples, if they would follow Him, they must take up their cross, and " cross " means, not burden, but death. Many disciples have been strengthened by the Holy Spirit to deaths of sacrificial love for the Lord and for men, and it is no detraction from the vicarious atonement of the Lord " for the sins of the world " that their deaths have been vicarious. They have died that man might be saved, and will be raised through the power of the same Holy Spirit dwelling in them (Rom. 8: 11).

Power Sufficient

This we need to remember when we are facing the fact that Jesus gave unto His Church the task of completing the work which He had begun. *The same power which equipped Him, He in turn bestowed upon the Church.*

This power was a mightier power than that of Satan, who was declared to be the prince of this world. Jesus had "entered his house," strong as he was, and had despoiled him of many of his possessions. He said this could not be done except the "strong man first be bound." Jesus had measurably bound Satan. Therefore, if there have been satanic forces in the world—and there have been—from that time to this, the Christian Church has the power that is greater than the power of Satan. We speak about entrenched evil. It has to become entrenched when the Church is assaulting it actively, for this is the only way it can exist.

Jesus did not undertake in His day radically to change conditions. He sent His disciples forth as sheep among wolves, and yet those sheep, again and again, defeated the wolves and lived where the wolves were done to death.

III. A PROGRAM WAS GIVEN TO THE CHURCH

The program given to the Church was not the program which the disciples desired. What an illuminating passage that is in the first chapter of Acts where it is said that the disciples came to Him and said, "Lord, wilt thou at this time restore again the kingdom of Israel?" Still, their mind was set upon their little country, a hundred and fifty miles long and fifty to seventy-five miles wide. They did not care for the rest of the world, except as it could minister unto them. They wanted to see the Roman power broken and the glory of Israel re-established as it was in the days of David and Solomon. No thought of a lost world yet filled their hearts. No vision of conquest of the vast Gentile world in the name of God gripped their souls. They had still the Judaistic self-centeredness in their minds, which was at once both the power and the weakness of the whole Judaistic system. They did not see that the time had come for the ripened pod of Hebrew concentration, which was Israel's genius, to be broken and the seed to be scattered far and wide in the whole earth.

Christ, in answer to their questions, blotted out the whole vision which they had and gave them again and, finally, the Great Commission for His Church. " Ye shall receive power after that the Holy Spirit is come upon you, and ye shall be witnesses unto me both in Jerusalem, and in all Judea, and Samaria, and unto the uttermost part of the earth." The program of the Church was that His disciples were to reproduce Him, represent Him unto the world. They were to be witnesses to what He was and did and said, and unto the power which He had bestowed upon them. They were to accomplish the same blessed works in the world and to spread the redemptive gospel which He had given. *The Church was to be the gigantic, spiritual manufacturing plant, and missions the product, the output* for the life of the world. It was to be the greatest business on earth.

The Way of Witnessing

How were Christ's disciples to be witnesses? First of all, by their lives, which had been changed through their contact with Him and through the filling of the Holy Spirit.

But now let us go back a little. Our Lord had said earlier to His Church-in-the-making, the embryonic Church, the disciples who were in a very short time to be the infant, and later the mature Church, " Ye are the salt of the earth." Not " some salt," not " part of the salt," but *the only salt* which the earth has. That was to be their function. What did He mean by that? Our Lord always used words with great discrimination.

Salt is a chemical of vast power—power to do two things. First of all, it gives a savor to our food. The little boy was right who, in response to the teacher's question as to what salt is, replied, " It is something that makes our potatoes taste bad when we don't put it in." Salt gives savor because the body needs it and welcomes it. The great purpose of Judaism in the world *was*, and the greater purpose of the Christian Church in the world *is*, to give savor or meaning to life. In heathenism and paganism the savor of life was lost. Life had become something meaningless, confused, insipid, so that the writer of the Book of Ecclesiastes, looking at life simply from the human point of view, concludes that life is utter " vanity and striving after wind "; and he proves that there is no meaning, no savor to life until one comes to the same conclusion that he reached: " Fear God and keep his commandments, for this is the whole of man." Thus true religion is that which gives meaning to life even after " desires fail."

How tragic it was that the great Greek philosophers, who reached heights of intellectual acumen and discovery not exceeded before or since, never found the true meaning of life; that Plato, the greatest of them all, perhaps the greatest human intellect that the world has ever seen, decided that the best thing in life was never to have been born, and the next best thing was an early death. This lack of savor so penetrated the Greek and Roman societies in the height of their glory that suicide was exceedingly common and life was considered very cheap.

But how different you find the meaning of life to have been among the devout Hebrews of the Old Testament! Go into the 103rd Psalm and with the Psalmist " bless Jehovah ": " Who forgiveth all thine iniquities, who healeth all thy diseases, who redeemeth thy life from destruction, who crowneth thee with loving kindness and tender mercies, who satisfieth thy mouth with good things, so that thy youth is renewed like the eagle." Here is life with a zest, and all because it is related to God. How glorious and meaningful was the life of Israel at its best, when it was serving God! They were the salt of the earth. They had the savor, and many were there of the heathen people who, like Ruth, joined their lot with theirs because of Jehovah, their God.

Saints Are Salt

And so the Christian Church was to give savor to life. It was thrust into the utterly vapid life of Greece and Rome after their glory had well-nigh departed; and it did reveal to them that life could have a glorious meaning. It came to be said by the heathen that it seemed that there was a new race among them—people with light in their eyes, and a smile upon their faces, and brightness radiating from them. As Christianity penetrated paganism, life took on vastly different values.

How greatly this is needed today! How terribly it was needed in Europe following the other war! A doctor who had studied in Vienna in the years following World War I told me that it was common in those days for whole families to commit suicide, so insipid and meaningless and terrible had life become. What is the significance of the vast increase in the number of suicides in our own land except that the salt is losing its savor, and that the Christian Church is not giving the deep, glorious, sweeping, colorful quality to life that it has been able to do in times of great revival? The craze for stimulants, narcotics, intoxicants, and thrills cries out the lack of meaning to life in America. Seeking " life " they are losing it.

But salt has another great power, and that is to prevent

or arrest corruption. Salt cannot turn putrid meat into that which is good and wholesome; but salt can prevent meat from becoming putrid, and it can arrest the putrefaction which is already begun. I was glad to find last summer that some pork rind that I once had cut into strips for fish bait and put in a bottle of strong brine and sealed tightly was just as good as when I put it there several years ago. Let this bottle remain sealed and the meat will be kept from spoiling indefinitely.

One part of the program of the Christian Church, therefore, is to arrest the forces of evil and to keep society from getting worse *while it saves those who can be saved*. People who seek to excuse themselves from using their power to arrest the forces of evil which are going on in their community are seeking to escape responsibility through Cain's dodge, " Am I my brother's keeper? " We are responsible not simply for what we do, but for what we might do; and when Christians have power, as they have in democratic America, to curb evil by right laws and efficient police powers, by education, sanitation, and discipline, they are themselves guilty when this is not done. The salt has largely lost its savor, and it is being cast out and trodden under foot of man. Men don't bother to damn the church any more. They just ignore it. They run over it heedlessly. The Church becomes impotent as a force of social righteousness when it might be powerful, and *it suffers tragically with the society which it has not saved* from the dominance of evils that might be curbed.

" Let There Be Light "

Again Jesus said, " Ye are the light of the world." Not some light, a kind of light, but *the only light* which is in the world; and in saying this He mentions something exceedingly more powerful even than salt.

Light not only shows the pathway so that we may not stumble in walking; light is one of the most generative powers, perhaps the most generative power in all the world. God is light. Jesus Christ is light. At a national conference of chemists in Chicago a few years ago, they decided that the ultimate element in this universe is light. Had they been religious enough, they would have concluded, then, that the ultimate element in the universe is God.

Now Jesus said to His disciples, " Ye are the light of the world," not a kind of light, one of many lights, but the only light! and the apostle Paul picked that up and declared that the early Christians were " luminaries," sources of light. We have not yet penetrated the full mystery of the generative power of light, but we do know that it calls forth the vegetation from the earth, which not only seeks the sun, but draws its life in some way from it. Dr. Henry E. Armstrong, writing on " The Chemical Romance of the Green Leaf " in *The Great Design*, says:

" The chloroplast is the seat of an astounding variety of operations. It combines within itself the activities of a brick works with those of the bricklayer. As the formaldehyde bricks are made with the aid of the sun, they are forthwith built into the form of walling we call starch."

And again,

" Life, as we see it, is an interplay of hydrone and carbon dioxide, begun under solar influence. . . . Plants and animals are all but machines working with solar energy."

So Christians have, through Christ, generative and regenerative power, the begetting of life and the renewing of life in the world. The power of Christians to draw by their very lives other people to Jesus Christ and into the Christian life is famous in Church history, ancient and modern. Christians are the very rays of Christ who lives in them and works through them.

But light has another terrific power that we are liable to forget. It is a destructive power, a power destructive of evil. It is perhaps the greatest germicide that we have discovered. Once we were told to fumigate the house with formaldehyde or sulphur to rid it of contagious diseases. Now they say that is not necessary. Open your house to the sunlight and the air, and the germs will speedily die.

Evil hates the light. Light kills it off. Men hated Jesus because He was such a blazing light. What boy has not turned up a stone and seen the creatures of darkness scurry as rapidly as they could crawl away from the blinding and disturbing light? In 1893, when the first World's Fair was in Chicago, I was a student in that city. One of the outstanding features of that Fair was the first mammoth searchlight of a million candlepower. Even before the Fair opened, this was trained night after night over that area of the city. One night I was walking along the street after midnight, and I confess I was walking out in the middle of the street, for the city had become so infested with thugs and hold-up men, getting ready for the unwary visitors to the Fair, that it was dangerous to be out at night. Suddenly I found myself in a blaze of light. The searchlight had been turned in that direction, and the whole area was swept with its glory, even though it was half a mile from the light. Did I dash into a dark doorway to escape the light? No, I exulted in it, for I knew that no evil man would dare to present himself in that radiant light. They hunted the darkness.

They Hate the Light

It is one great function of the Christian Church to be such a blaze of light in the community that evil shall hide. A number of years ago the city of New York had become an acknowledged cesspool of protected iniquity. Its political life was in the control of the very worst of men. Graft and crime and evil of every kind abounded unchecked, and the police force, sent to restrain evil, protected it because of the " hush money " which was paid to them. The city seemed utterly hopeless of ever getting out of this enslaved condition. Then Dr. Charles H. Parkhurst, the great Presbyterian preacher, started to lift up his voice against the brazen political and social devilishness. But his was a voice crying in the wilderness. No one paid heed to it until he himself, with his son-in-law, started into the detective business on their own. Disguised, they went down through the haunts of vice and crime, which anyone could get into if one went at it the right way. They got their devastating facts in great abundance and then Dr. Parkhurst blazed them forth, so that something had to be done. Action against the evil was started. During all of the great campaign he and others carried on, he went forward week by week preaching great sermons. In one of them he said, " While it is true that ' the wicked fleeth when no man pursueth,' I notice that he makes vastly better time if a righteous man is after him." The result of turning on the light was that the city became aroused and, finally, there was reformation after reformation, until New York became a fairly well governed city, even in spite of Tammany Hall.

In the days before prohibition we were fighting the saloon. The best method proved to be the " Springfield plan." The city of Springfield, Massachusetts, of about ninety thousand, coped with the problem of law enforcement in this way: The citizens organized themselves to get the facts and blaze them abroad. They did not undertake to enforce the law themselves, but they got the facts and then published them week by week in a little paper called " The Frozen Truth," stating just what was going on in a certain building upon a certain corner; and with these hot rays of light the officials had to get busy, and they did clean up the city. Light is something which evil fears, and it is that which the Church is commissioned to shed and to be shedding all the time. Just how the Church is to do this work of turning the light upon social evil we will consider in a later chapter.

" The Gospel—The Power of God "

The disciples were to be witnesses by their Gospel, which was given unto them, as well as by their lives. Paul perceived the Gospel to be the power of God unto salvation to those who believed, and the special commission of the Church was to proclaim that Gospel. To be a witness to Christ was to testify not only to the fact of His being, to the life that He lived, to the general teachings which He gave, but especially to His atoning death and to His resurrection by which men could be justified from their sins. This has been the great power of the Christian Church, the power of its revelation of redemption. We will understand better how it has accomplished what it has done by noting the scientific way in which it has worked from individuals to community, from souls to society, from conversions to civilizations.

The first effect of the Gospel, when it is received, is to *change the human heart*—understanding heart to mean, as it does in the Bible, the essential personality, not simply the affections, but the will and the mental processes. " If any man be in Christ, he is a new creature " is not only a dogmatic statement of the apostle Paul, but is a record of history. When the sins are laid on Jesus; when the love of self gives way to the love of God; when the rebellious will is surrendered to the lordship of Jesus Christ; when the whole philosophy, the mainspring of life, is changed, then one indeed is born anew, regenerated, re-created, a new creature. Since this re-creating power is above us, one is born " from above." This is the experience of all who have actually received the Gospel. It proves to be the power of God to change the personality.

When the heart is changed, then *the habits of life become changed*. This is the evidence and proof of the change of heart. The habit of prayerlessness is changed to the habit of prayer, the habit of profanity is transformed into a habit of reverence. The name of God which was taken carelessly and in vain is now taken soberly and with an exalted purpose. Habits of worldliness are changed to habits of worship. Habits of the association with the godless give way to fellowship with the godly. Habits of carnality are sloughed off, and habits of spirituality are seen in their place. How nearly complete the change of heart is will be registered by the degree in which the whole habits of life are cast into a new mold. Do not trust any professed conversion that does not produce a changed life.

With the heart and the habits changed, there is bound to be effected a *change in the home*, especially if the one whose heart has been changed is one of the dominant factors in the family. But even where this person apparently may be a very minor factor in the home, such as a young child or a servant, again and again has a whole home life been transformed by the witness of this one with changed heart and habits. Sometimes resistance and even persecution are manifested on the part of the others of the home, and yet the history of Christianity reveals that even these persecuted and resisted ones have, in the end, proved often to be a mighty alembic in the crucible of the home life. On our mission fields a little child attending a kindergarten has carried the Gospel songs and stories home, and later we have often found that this has revolutionized the life of the whole household. Often in a striking way this is seen in the Christian Centers in our homeland. A consecrated woman, directing such a Center among the Negroes in one of our large northern cities, tells of a family—a father and mother and nine children—who represented life on a very low scale, even among the Negroes. One of the little girls started to come to the Christian Center. The beauty of the place and of Jesus, who was central in the teachings there given and who thus made this a true Christian Center, began quickly to show its effect upon her. She carried this influence back to her home. Later she brought a brother and then a sister. Soon the mother came to the Center to see what it was that was having such a beautiful effect upon her children. The light and the love and the warmth and the power of the Gospel reached her heart. She brought the rest of the children and her husband, who had been a dissipated man; and it was not long until this whole home was a new home in every way—so new that we find the next great transition.

There has come naturally the *change of habitation*, when hearts, habits, and homes have been changed. A careful study of the history of Christianity would reveal that Christian habitations are something entirely distinct from heathen abodes throughout. Many Christians, it is true, have lived in hovels and many pagans in palaces; but there would be little trouble in distinguishing something unique, clean, and wholesome about the houses of genuine Christians. This has been greatly marked on our foreign mission fields. Dr. Henry P. Van Dusen, in that remarkable book of his, *For the Healing of the Nations*, written as a result of a tour by himself and his wife to study missions first-hand before partaking in the Madras Conference, has told how striking was the difference between the dwelling places, without and within, of the Christians in the pagan isles which he visited. I myself have seen that in the lands where our Gospel has been doing its glorious transforming work. Cleanliness, sanitation, the separation of the sexes at night, the things which make for decency and comfort—these are a striking fruitage of Christian homes.

Now, it naturally follows that when enough hearts, habits, homes, and habitations have been changed by the Gospel, you will find whole *hamlets* to be distinctively Christian. Rev. Brayton Case of Pyinmana, Burma, has pointed out how whole villages, which had become Christian, no longer had the constant contest with crime, no longer had to have policemen patrol the streets day and night, no longer had the carousing of the inebriated. The village itself was converted! We visited the hamlet of Kongole in Burma, where half of the population were Christians. It was a village of about four hundred, situated in one of the best agricultural areas of Burma. When the people became Christian, they gravitated together; and therefore the hamlet was divided in a very marked way between the Christian section and the pagan. In the Christian part the houses were of better construction in every way. Most of them were surrounded by a fence. They had trees and shrubs and flowers. The whole aspect of the village reflected thrift and a new sense of beauty. We, with the missionaries, had taken our breakfast with us, though we were told that we could safely eat with the family in the home which we visited. Everything was clean—the food was clean. We were told that we could safely put our sun hats on the couch, and that when we took them up, there would be no more in them than when we laid them down—something unusual in the Orient! Eating breakfast Sunday morning about eight o'clock, we heard singing and were told it was the early morning prayer meeting over at the little church. I went there and found about a hundred and twenty-five of the two hundred Christians had come together. At nine o'clock the women were to have their special prayer meeting. At ten the men would reassemble for a prayer meeting of their own. At eleven they all came together for the church service, and I was permitted to preach to them through the interpreter. Following the church service we made a tour of the heathen part of the village. No Gospel service could be held there in the afternoon, because the people were mostly out in the fields guarding their rice harvest. But we went through the streets in that part of the village. The people owned just as good land as the Christians', and were just as well-to-do; but the contrast was striking to the last degree. There was not a fence about a home; there was not a tree; there was not a flower. Pigs rooted under the houses, and in some places chickens were in the house. In so far as we could look into the homes there was uncleanness and confusion. They were heathen houses all right, the abodes of people with untransformed hearts and habits.

In my boyhood days I saw the transforming power of Christianity in a pioneer town in the West. My people had moved into a new section of the Dakotas, ahead of the railway and of the survey. When the railroad came through they platted a town near us. Immediately the little villages, which had mushroomed in that area, hoping the railroad would strike them, moved to this new town site. And now in came the saloons, in came the gamblers, in came the harlots, in came the cowboys at night to drink and shoot up the town until it was " wild and woolly " indeed. But also in came the Christian people to organize their churches and soon to build places of worship. I saw the fine group of Christian people proceed to dominate the life of that community, the genuine taxpayers to get control of the town and county offices, the elements of vice and crime to be driven out or brought under strict control; and out from that little town has gone, in the years since, a stream of educated, cultured Christian young men and women. That hamlet was transformed by Christians, not so completely as it ought to have been, but measurably so.

Now, when you get enough hamlets changed by the Gospel, why not expect *whole hemispheres* to be transformed? And that is what has happened. Though South America has in it a vast amount of baptized paganism in the name of Roman Catholicism, North and South America, in comparison, stand immeasurably ahead of Asia and Africa in the things of cultured and clean and fruitful society.

When we realize what the Gospel has done, even with the perversions which have come into the Christian Church, we are bound to realize that, had the Church remained pure, had hearts and habits and homes been completely under the power of the pure Word of God, had His people always been salt that had not lost its savor, and light not hid under bushels of selfishness, cowardice, and neglect, we would have seen in an even more striking degree national and international conditions steadily improved, as have those smaller areas where the Gospel has been dominant.

Think of Hernnhut, the city of the Moravians, with the whole community from youth to old age glorified by the Gospel! We see in them what all society should have been where the Christians were dominant. Pure Christianity, working under the power of Christ, changes social units and thus society; and it was sent to do this. It is thus that people are saved out of the world while in the world by being brought into the Kingdom of God, which has come near. Whether one believes that Christ came to make civilizations or not, He most certainly has done so, as we shall see.

We are not sent " to bring in the Kingdom." That can be brought in in its fullness and power, only by the King Himself when He comes. But since He has brought the essentials of the Kingdom near, namely, the love of God and the rule of God for all who will submit; and since He has sent the Church to call people to enter into that " Kingdom of the Son of his love," which Paul says the Colossians had been translated into, we should expect the " rule of God," which is His Kingdom, accepted here and now, to bear its fruit in human society, in " righteousness, peace and joy in the Holy Ghost." *There is no social gospel;* let us use language right. There are social duties, but duties are not good news. *But neither is there any genuine Gospel which does not bear the social fruits of righteousness.* " And the fruit of righteousness shall be peace." This was the purpose with which the Church was launched in the power of the Holy Ghost.

The Church has had the power to carry out its purpose to bless and to improve immeasurably world conditions; therefore the Church has a vast responsibility for the present world conditions, both good and bad.

III

CHRISTIANITY'S RESPONSIBILITY FOR THE GOOD IN THE WORLD

And he answered and said, He that soweth the good seed is the Son of man; the field is the world; and the good seed are the children of the Kingdom; and the tares are the children of the wicked one.—MATTHEW 13: 37–38.

THERE is a vast amount of good in the world today. No one will deny this, or that good is found in every land, in the non-Christian, the heathen lands, as well as in the Christian. The Son of God is " the true light which lighteth every man that cometh into the world." That which we call conscience is the unidentified Christ mercifully left in men to bring them to the full light. It is the ground of the work of Christianity. Paul recognizes that " for as many as have sinned without law shall also perish without law; and as many as have sinned in the law shall be judged by the law."

But the world was rapidly decaying when Christianity was injected into it. By this time, if Christianity had not come to arrest the decay and to plant the germs of new life, the good largely would have disappeared from the earth. Greek and Roman society was corrupting rapidly. *Quo Vadis* gave a true picture of the sensuality which abounded in Rome in the days when Peter is supposed to have visited there, and, according to the story, to have started to leave the city when Christ met him and turned him back. The very conditions revealed in the Corinthian Church show what a cesspool these people had been lifted from by the Gospel. In heathen lands in the Far East decay was going on rapidly. One of the proofs that degeneration, rather than evolution, has marked the history of humanity is in the fact that the earlier religions of the heathen lands were far less impure than the later. The books of India that have been translated and printed, the Upanishads and the Vedas, in which occur so many noble sentiments that Edwin Arnold was caused to write "The Light of Asia," all belong to the dim and distant past. Most of the later writings of the Hindu religion, with some notable exceptions, such as the Bhagavd-Gita, are so foul that they are absolutely untranslatable. Such writers as Tagore are largely the product of the impact of Christian truth as it has infiltrated into society there. He, like the moon, shone with reflected light.

The restraining effect of Christianity, even where it has not brought a transformation, is revealed in the way in which heathenism has sloughed off some of its more abominable practices since Christian missions have entered the lands. The heathen ideals and practices depicted by William Ward, the companion of Carey, in his rare book, *A View of the History, Literature, and Religion of the Hindoos,* are far more degraded and awful than are found in that land today. Not only has the burning of widows been prohibited, and the throwing of little babes into the Ganges river been discontinued, but in many another way heathenism has reformed because of the very presence of the higher ideals of the Christian religion; and the good which you find in the heathen lands today can be credited very largely to the light which has shone over the earth, dimly indeed in many places, from the cross of Christ.

But where Christianity has gone as a mighty stream into

the Western world, and to some extent toward the East, transformations have been great and glorious.

> " Blessings abound where'er He reigns,
>   The prisoner leaps to lose his chains,
>   The weary find eternal rest,
>   And all the sons of want are blessed."

This stanza in Watts' famous hymn, " Jesus Shall Reign," is a true summary of the effect of the Gospel. The blessings of freedom, of soul rest, and of economic advance are clearly marked in our Lord's stride across the Western world. He has made that which is good in our civilization.

T. R. Glover, in his *Christian Tradition and Its Verification*,* draws the striking picture of what the world would be without Christ, saying:

" Most of us have no idea at all what the world is without Christ; He is so deeply involved in every aspect of the world we know, so interwoven with every fiber of its being. . . . Deplorable as things are in European and American society, they are bad, nevertheless, with the continual correction of a Christian background. There are men and women governing these societies in whom burns a passionate devotion to the person of Jesus Christ and His ideals for mankind as for individuals. There is the public recognition of religion, and there is in all educated persons some slight knowledge, very vague and inaccurate as it may be, of the principles of that religion which touches their lives, if nowhere else, in most of their weddings and funerals. But imagine the background removed. And industrial enormities, flagrant cruelties, and open uncleanness continuing unchecked, and gaining rather than losing in volume, as they would. Even with the assistance of Leopold II and his Belgians [this was written at a time of the Belgian atrocities in the Congo] it will be hard for anyone to imagine what things were tolerated in ancient society—or are tolerated in India—in civilized communities, that is, and in neither case with much

* The Macmillan Company, pp. 60–62.

disapproval. Some things are ignored and others defended; and that makes an unspeakable difference. Good natures and kind hearts there were in the ancient world, but it is remarkable how little influence they had. Classical scholars and modern missionaries rarely tell us all they know about pagan society. . . . Then we must think about religion without Christ. Here, of course, we meet people who go at once to the diary of Marcus Aurelius or Sir Edwin Arnold's 'Light of Asia,' documents of very different value; but there are sounder works on Buddha with less glamour, while Marcus Aurelius was in any case an exceptional man. Plutarch's book *On Isis and Osiris* is a much better guide to the real ideas of ancient religion." *

But now let us take an airplane ride across the centuries and see in some of the lofty ranges of culture what the Gospel has done in the way of blessing the world.

I. THE LORD'S WORK WAS GERMINAL

Our Lord wrought no great social changes, neither did He undertake any as such. His healing and His helping of individuals was secondary to His great purpose of preaching the Gospel. He very definitely refused to follow the program for radical social and political changes which some even of His disciples, like Simon the Zealot, wanted Him to undertake.

With Him the Gospel was primary. He was for laying a right foundation. He was sowing seed. In His parable of the wheat and the tares He said that the good seed are the children of the Kingdom, and He was the one who was sowing this good seed. This parable, rather than the parable of the leaven, indicates how He expected His Gospel to change society. The parable of the leaven has been misinterpreted by those who have not been careful with their historical, grammatical, and logical exegesis. In every other place in the Bible leaven is used in a bad sense, indicating

* Quoted by permission.

FIRST BAPTIST CHURCH
16TH & "O" STS., N. W.
WASHINGTON 6, D. C.

ferment and decay, and we cannot conceive of His hearers thinking of what He said in that day in any other light than that the Church would be perverted by evil, as, indeed, we shall see later, following the days of the apostles, it was.

But there can be no question what He meant when He said, " The good seed are the children of the kingdom." Christians are not simply saved people; they also are seed for further sowing and therefore for saving others. A seed is something which springs up into life and bears fruit, and that fruit contains abundant seed for other crops. The surest test of your Christianity and of mine is in this: Suppose that all Christians in the world except you or me should be blotted out in some great catastrophe. Would Christianity take a fresh start from you in the world? Would it take a fresh start from me? Would you prove to be vital seed, so that from you other Christians would be produced? Or would Christianity die out with you? This is the abundant life which He gave—life which is reproductive as well as glorious in itself.

When the Lord sowed this good seed, the " children of the kingdom," He put something into society, some sources of great ideals, a new concept of human worth and of human society. He laid the foundation for vast social changes as well as, and because of, individual changes.

II. THE EARLY CHURCH REVEALS THE PROGRESS OF THE GOSPEL

The first Christians began, indeed, with no set purpose to change society. They went out with the Gospel and with their own changed lives. The burden of their testimony was " Jesus and the resurrection "—a blessed fact and a blessed hope. They gave no immediate attention to social changes— neither the humble individual Christians nor the apostles themselves.

In his recent remarkable book, *The Social Message of the Apostle Paul,* Dr. Holmes Rolston points out both the conservative and the radical elements in the teaching of Paul. His immediate teachings were in every case conservative. He undertook no revolution in society which then existed or in the state. He urged slaves to be obedient to their masters, Christian wives to be subservient to their husbands, children to obey their parents, citizens to be obedient unto the government as it was. Yet, on the other hand, his teachings abound with ideals that were radical and revolutionary, and they proved to be so when they began to work out sufficiently through the lives of those who had become Christians. Anyone who has followed at all the political and social history of the early Christian centuries in the Western world must see that the change in hearts, habits, and homes eventually wrought mighty transformations in the social and political life of the age. Conditions were affected in every area touched by the Early Church. The epistles reveal not perfect conditions, but rapidly changing conditions.

The apparently simple and brief statement of the duties, from the Christian point of view, of the six social classes—husbands and wives, parents and children, employed and employers—which Paul gives us in Ephesians and Colossians, has in it the dynamic of an utterly new social life. In fact, if the little which Paul has said in these letters should be adopted absolutely wherever the Gospel has gone, there would be a complete and blessed transformation of society over night. The early Christians began to change society because they were changed. The seed began to produce a new social as well as individual growth.

III. THE GOSPEL WROUGHT REVOLUTIONS IN EUROPE

Many people still say that they do not believe in missions. Some will tell us that they " believe in home missions, but not in foreign missions "; and from the way they say it, you can know that their view of the home mission field which they are interested in is exceedingly narrow and circumscribed, that they themselves are in the center of it.

All these people need in order to change their point of view is to see what Christian missions have done for their ancestors and thus for them. Most Americans have sprung from European forebears. What were our ancestors in northern Europe before the Gospel was brought to them? Look squarely at them, and say if you would want to be like them.

For many years our Christian missionaries in China made very little headway. The cultured Chinese would say, " What business have you coming over here and teaching us? When your ancestors were naked and horrid savages in the north of Europe, we already had a civilization a thousand years old." And they were right. Before Augustine and the other Christian missionaries came to England, our English forebears were offering human sacrifices. The Druids, according to Diodorus Siculus, " used human victims for their divinations." I know of no heathen today who are shedding human blood as a religious rite, except in a few remote parts of Assam, where, unrestrained by the government, they feel that human blood is necessary to fertilize their fields. Our Scandinavian countries have been in recent years the centers of a great, stable, and glorious culture. Before Hitler set his murderous heel down upon it, little Denmark had gone farther toward solving the problem of the equitable distribution of the products of the earth than any other country, and yet, before Ansgar and other missionaries came to Scandinavia, the ancestors of our splendid Scandinavian people, mighty, savage, and lustful, would drink upon occasion, it is said, the blood of their enemies, thinking to get the spirit and the power of the enemy into themselves. I know of no savages so low today that they even drink their enemies' blood with any such purpose. Those who have Scotch ancestry can well be proud of the bonnie land of Scotland that has sent forth more preachers and missionaries in proportion to population than any other land, and yet, before Christian missions carried the Gospel to Scotland, cannibalism, I have read, was practiced there. I know of no cannibalism existing in the world today, except in some of the remote recesses of Africa. What were the Celts of Ireland and the Welsh before the Gospel got to them? Horrible enough, so that one can be thankful that Patrick took the Gospel to Ireland, and that early missionaries carried it to Wales. Ulfilas started the Gospel work that lifted the savages of Germany into sainthood.

In other words, he who says that he does not believe in foreign missions is saying that he does not believe in himself. He does not believe in what has made his mother the glorious woman she is and in what has brought protection to little children.

Years ago, G. Loring Brace wrote a striking book entitled *Gesta Chrsiti*, Latin for the *Deeds of Christ*, in which he traced the effect of Christianity upon the social life of the Roman Empire. Recently the far abler and more conclusive book *Anno Domini*,* by Prof. Kenneth Scott Latourette, traces the influence of Jesus through the centuries. A few paragraphs from this remarkable, lucid and convincing book will show how Christianity, which started out conveying the good news from person to person, very rapidly effected wide and deep social changes:

" Christianity destroyed or weakened certain features of Græco-Roman culture. It eliminated the ancient official cults. It brought to an end the pagan schools of philosophy. It denied the divinity of the emperor. It challenged the authority

* The Macmillan Company, p. 50. Quoted by permission.

of the state to the complete control of the conscience of the Christian. It assisted in the modification of the type of labor, slavery, which was an integral part of the economic structure of the Græco-Roman society. . . .

" From Jesus, moreover, through Christianity, was derived the impulse which led to the creation of much that was finest in that which was new in thought, in literature, and in art, and which, by its high moral ideals, troubled the conscience of the peoples who built the new cultures and haunted and inspired them with a vision of what human life might mean. . . .[1]

" In the sixth century the Institutes of Justinian show innovation in the regulations of marriage, in respect to chastity, and relating to the exposure of infants, which are in the direction of the ethics of Jesus. . . .[2]

" To the monasteries, too, were due the encouragement of some of the simpler handicrafts and many improvements in agriculture and in varieties of fruit and breeds of cattle. . . . Much of the early banking was done by ecclesiastical bodies. The Church was the first to accumulate reserves of capital, took the lead in advocating a stable coinage, and instituted the system of deposits. The Templars were famous as bankers. In the theory of property teachers who professed to be seeking the Christian ideal held that God is the owner of all and that individual men simply hold wealth in trust. . . .[3]

" Upon marriage and the life of the family Jesus had an effect. Following what is believed to be His commands, the Church stood for monogamy and against polygamy and against concubinage, and made divorce difficult. The honors paid to the virgin probably helped to give dignity to womanhood. Perhaps, too, the celebration of the nativity and the Christmas carols, which arose out of it, tended to give sanctity to conception and child-bearing and to inculcate respect for childhood."[4]

Marvelous have been the transformations wrought by the Gospel. The whole fabric of Western civilization is shot

[1] *Ibid.*, p. 52.
[2] *Ibid.*, p. 72.
[3] *Ibid.*, p. 92.
[4] *Ibid.*, p. 98.

through with its gracious influences. Individuals are the units of society and the parts cannot be changed without the whole being renewed.

Dr. Endicott, secretary of Foreign Missions for the United Church in Canada, gave a great address at the Northern Baptist Convention in St. Louis in 1936. As he began, he held a New Testament in his hand and said that in his recent reading of the New Testament he had noticed that, while the first four books all have to do with the home country of Palestine, the home towns and the home personalities, the moment one gets out of them into the fifth book, the Book of Acts, one begins to deal with foreign peoples and foreign missions. In the second chapter of Acts, seventeen nationalities are mentioned, and from that time on the rest of the New Testament is made up of letters and documents written by foreign missionaries to foreign mission churches. From that he traced the progress of the Gospel up through Europe, which produced, as we have seen, not only the fruit of changed lives, but the fruit of reformed society.

IV. THE GOSPEL IN AMERICA WROUGHT THE SAME GLORIOUS EFFECT

The Puritans landed in America, not to improve their physical condition, but to have liberty to serve God in the freedom and the light of the Gospel. They were essentially missionaries, although they did not come here primarily to evangelize the natives. They did come to plant a godly community, a Christian society. They were clearly sent of God, and to be sent means to be a missionary. They came to establish the ripened fruit of the Gospel in Church and State. Roger Williams and his friends carried this much farther than did the Puritans, and both evangelized the Indians and established the political product of the Gospel in a democracy which recognized the absolute freedom of the Church from the power of the State. In this they were assisted by the Quakers. The Baptists of Virginia were the ones, according to Bishop Hurst and other reliable historians, who, after suffering severe persecution at the hand of the Church of England for preaching without ecclesiastical license, started the agitation which resulted in the first amendment to the Constitution guaranteeing religious liberty. There was no specific command by Christ or the apostles envisaging anything like this, but the seeds which Christ planted in the new soil were rooted also in the ideas of freedom which had developed through the centuries, and they bore this fruit of separation of Church and State in America. As there is not only an oak but a forest in every acorn, so there is a family, a church, a community, a state, a civilization potentially in every Christian.

When we look, then, to the evangelism of the new land which the early Christians undertook at once, first of the Indians, then of the pioneers as they crossed the Alleghanies, on into the Mississippi Valley and then beyond—the work of John Mason Peck and a host of other intrepid home missionaries—we see how the Gospel has been woven into the very fabric of our national life and how our American civilization at its best has grown from and been molded by the Gospel; and all the changed conditions which we have welcomed and gloried in, bringing us comfort and social peace, are just the legitimate fruitage of the purpose, power, and program of the Christian Church launched by our Lord.

To quote again from Professor Latourette, " It is important to notice, moreover, that in opposing the selfish exploitation of the weaker by the stronger races, the impulses from Jesus were much more effective in the three hundred years after 1500 than they had been in the previous thousand years." It was greatly effective here in America.

We can trace the effect of the program and of the power

of Christianity into the physical blessings which we here in the Western world enjoy. Thomas A. Edison, so far as I know, never admitted that there is a God. Toward the close of his life he did admit that there might be life after death. But Edison never could have given us the electric lights and the other blessings of electricity in any other civilization than one made stable and prosperous by Christianity. It is no accident that the great era of inventions is the Christian era. It is no accident that the great section of the world which has been blessed by modern inventions is the section of the world where the Gospel has been so dominant. One of the members of my church, a Scotchman, visited a few years ago his old mother on the north coast of Scotland. He found the town about as it was when he was a boy. Upon his return he called at our home. My wife said to him that she was sure his mother hated to see him come away, and he replied, " Oh, yes, I guess she did. But she said, anyway, that she would be free from my everlasting lying." When asked what the mother meant, he said that he had simply told her what we had over here in America—buildings ten, twenty, thirty, forty stories high, and that we ran our street-cars and lighted our homes, cooked our food, cooled the food, and the women did the washing and ironing, and even curled their hair with electricity; and she would protest, " Begone with your everlasting lying." But we know that he was not lying. He was telling of how in a material way a land had been blessed by the wealth which was started by Christianity and by the faith of our stable society.

One night on a Pullman train, when I was going to a meeting of the Foreign Mission Society, as a last thing before sleeping, I started to pray. There came into my mind, and I said it, " Oh, Lord, Thou didst never lie down in such a comfortable bed as this in all Thy earthly life." I thought of the hard pallets on the floor where He had slept, and of the nights in which He had lain out upon the hard ground underneath the stars; and for a few moments I felt ashamed of myself to be going to a missionary meeting in such luxury. And then something else came to my mind, and I said it, " But, Lord, I have this comfort, this luxury, and all of the other luxuries of life, because Thou didst suffer on Calvary and because Thy Gospel flowing down through the centuries has made possible all the blessed and glorious civilization which we have." Any thoughtful person will know that I was right in what I said, and we ought daily to remember this.

Our very democracy is the fruitage of Christianity. It was the Lord who revealed the immeasurable worth of the individual, and that all men are equal as personalities before God and are equally precious to Him. Therefore they should be equal before one another. Robert Burns' famous poem, " A Man's a Man for A' That," is an outburst of Christian thought. Plato's *Republic* never even glimpsed the glory of the ballot in the hand of every man and woman—the scepter of power wielded by them. It is our democracy, the highest form of government known to man, that has made possible that freedom of life and that interrelation of activities and that unlimited opportunity for the lowliest individual which have worked together to produce the America that we love.

And when one thinks of the social blessings, especially those which have come to women and children, in our land, we must realize that they are the fruit of the Gospel, the work of missions. To look at the state of womanhood and childhood before the coming of Christ and at their state today in lands where He has not come in the fulness of His power, is to look upon a most tragic and pitiable picture. No prediction was ever more literally fulfilled than that made in Eden to Eve, " Thy desire shall be to thy husband and he shall rule over thee." Formerly women were the sad and abused slaves of men. It is Jesus who has touched womanhood and restored it to the beauty of Eden before the Fall and to feminine freedom. It is Jesus who made history turn on its hinges when He took a little child and set it in the midst of the disciples.

One time, after visiting a patient in a city hospital, I stopped at the door of the children's ward, as it was in those days, where were cribs and beds for children all the way from two years down to the section where there were the little ones who had just ventured into the world. As I stood at the door and looked upon that scene of protected childhood, a nurse came along, and seeing my interest said, " Here is the littlest one." I turned and saw that she had a bundle in her arm. She drew back the coverlet, and I saw a little face not much bigger than a dollar. She said, " It weighed less than two pounds when it was born." This was before the days of incubators. And then she said with a thrill of prospective triumph, " I think we shall yet win out." My mind leaped back over the centuries to Greece and Rome at the time of their greatest glory, when a little mite like that would have been cast out to the dogs. In those days a newborn babe was laid at the feet of the father. If the father deigned to look down on the baby, it was taken and nursed, and given a chance for life; if he did not look down on it, it was taken and cast out by a servant into the hills, there to die of exposure, to be eaten by the dogs or wolves, or to be picked up by a shepherd to be reared as another slave. But in the hospital not the Church but the State was fighting for the life of this little mite of humanity and glorying in the possibility of helping it to live.

One of our missionaries from Africa said that the people among whom he labored were literally bushmen. When the time came for a babe to be born, it was born out in the bush. No loving hands came and took the woman tenderly to a hospital where they would, with science and sympathy, care for her and her babe. She went off alone into the jungle, far enough from the village so that her cries could not be heard. If she returned with a living babe, well and good; but if not, one or two more bodies were off there in the jungle to be devoured by the animals. Look upon womanhood and childhood in America, and then not thank God for Christian missions—if you can!

Compare America and India. Katherine Mayo has shown that many of the worst evils of the people of India are not in spite of their religion, as in this country, but because of their religion. The little child must be married at a very tender age because no woman can be saved until she is married to a man. And how they have fought the raising of the lower age limit of marriage from ten to twelve and then to fourteen years. But look at these two countries on the lowest plane, the physical. India has a population of four hundred million. A hundred million of them are always on the verge of starvation—not simply hungry, but near starving. One missionary has told that men in the rural area where he was had but one real meal a day, and that was millet seed. At night a man will soak a double handful of it in water. In the morning he will wrap it up in his turban and put it on top of his head. He then goes out to work under that boiling sun. At noon he will take down this milet seed, now fairly thoroughly stewed, and fill his stomach with it. We use it for chicken feed and cattle feed in this country. There humans are sustained by it. Another hundred million people have never known what you and I know three times a day—the sense of a full stomach. They are never heard to remark, " Oh, I've eaten too much." Dr. Timpany, many years a missionary in India, said to his wife before they started on a furlough that he was going to give the native Christian men all the rice they could eat for once. So he invited in two hundred and fifty of them and told them what he had planned. The rice was cooked in great kettles, with a little curry put over it. It was served on plantain-leaves as large as our rhubarb leaves; and, as Mrs. Timpany illustrated, the helping was as much as you could stack on a dinner plate. Many of the men ate that amount three times, after which they looked literally like brownies, with their spindly legs and arms, and their stomachs sticking out over the huge quantity of rice that they had crammed inside of them. She protested to her husband that the feast would kill them. He said, " Kill them! They've been starving for three hundred years. They will absorb all you can get inside of their skins."

Why all of this poverty in India as against the plenty in America? Such abundance have we that in the time of depression we found that there was no man, woman, or child in America that needed to go hungry or be without shelter or clothing. We were able to care for them all. It is not because of our " rocks and rills, our woods and templed hills "; it is not because of our

> " Amber waves of grain
> And purple mountain majesties,
> Above the fruited plain."

India is as rich in natural resources as is America. The real reason is that we have had the Gospel for centuries and our forebears for centuries before us, and India, as a people, has never yet had the Gospel.

We are in a very true sense a Christian nation in that the ideals which are dominant among us are the ideals which came from Christ. We could trace the blessing along every artery of our national life. Even those who do not believe in the Bible have been blessed by the Bible. Even those

who reject Christ have been blessed by His Gospel. He is
in the very fabric of our society. Atheists and agnostics
cannot escape Him. He has built our states, formed our
governing bodies, made our laws, built our railroads and fac-
tories, lighted our cities and homes, founded our schools,
printed our books and papers, bound us together in a great
commonwealth, where the *wealth* is *common* as in no other
land. Above all, He has built our churches and made for
us a great Christian fellowship.

V. THE FRUIT OF THE GOSPEL IN ASIA AND AFRICA IS MANIFEST

In Asia and Africa we see the Gospel's transforming power,
not simply in the lives of individuals but in whole communities. When John G. Paton went to the New Hebrides,
it was a land of cannibalism. He and his fellow missionaries
had to get out of the country one time to save their lives,
but they went back and persisted in bringing the Gospel to
those debased people. Before Paton came to the end of his
notable life, the British government listed the New Hebrides
in its Blue Book as the best governed spot on the earth,
freest from crime and debasing influences. Those who have
read Belle Brain's *The Transformation of Hawaii*, now, un-
fortunately, long out of print, will remember the glorious
picture of the triumphs of the Gospel there. When the
Congregational missionaries first went to the Hawaiian Islands, the people were at the lowest level of heathenism.
They had had some little contact with white men through
the voyages of Cook and others and had picked up a smat-
tering of some of the superficial elements of civilized life.
The first time the king and his several wives came to call
upon the new missionaries, they revealed their spiritual
destitution in that they came clothed in nothing but the
brilliant sunshine of that land. It was suggested to them

that they would be more acceptable if they would clothe themselves, and the next time the king came to call, he himself had on a pair of women's stockings and a high hat that he had found discarded by some of the white people. No clothing was supposed to be necessary for his wives. But after fifty years the Congregationalists withdrew their missionaries, because the whole island had been evangelized, Christianized, and civilized. They made a great mistake in thus withdrawing, for very soon afterwards came the great influx of Chinese and Japanese and other Orientals. The local churches could not cope with this, and the island rapidly became paganized and has largely continued so to this day, so far as these Oriental elements are concerned.

Dr. Henry P. Van Dusen gives in his book already referred to, *For the Healing of the Nations,* a thrilling account of what Christianity has done in the East Indian Islands. One of our missionaries to Africa has stated that he has seen the lowest savages become ladies and gentlemen in one generation, a feat for which evolution, if working at what some suppose to be its best, would need a million years.

Professor Latourette, in speaking of the mission for the Indians of southern Chile, carried on by the son and grandson of Captain Gardiner, the intrepid pioneer of missions in the lowest part, socially as well as geographically, of South America, says, " Charles Darwin was so impressed with the achievements registered among peoples whom he had regarded as hopelessly degraded that he became a regular contributor to the funds of the society." * There is the story of an anthropological expedition sailing around Cape Horn and refusing to stop at the island of Tierra del Fuego because of the conviction that its inhabitants were not above the animal stage. It is said that on the very day in which they doubled the Horn and refused to give any consideration to

* *The Great Century,* p. 104, Harper and Brothers.

these " sub-humans," as they were considered to be, a babe
was born in London who was destined later to become a
missionary to that very island, and to see there the transforming power of the Gospel lift those degraded human beings up to the high level of spiritual Christians.

We were in a home in China by invitation of an aged
woman. It was a humble home, but clean and sweet in every
way. The woman who had invited us was in the eighties,
and was seated in a chair when we came to see her. Her
face had that glorious serenity and Christian beauty of my
grandmother. With her that day was her son who for thirty
years had been the fine Christian cook for one of our missionary families. Three grandsons aged ten, twelve, and
fifteen, in the uniform of the Academy at Swatow, were also
present. The youngest boy held in his hand a large picture, which I shall tell you about later. Who was this
woman? She had at one time been a beggar on the streets
of Swatow, and beggars in that part of China beggar all
description. It is said that a Chinese gentleman in this
country was asked whether it was literally true that people in China ate rats. He was wise enough to parry this
with another question, whether it was really true that in
America the people ate hot dogs. Under the laugh which this
question aroused, he escaped, and it was well for him that
he did; for, in this section of China, the missionary told me,
the theory was that anything which had had life could support
life. We had an exhibition of the truth of that philosophy.
One evening, as we were crossing the compound, we saw two
young men with a bamboo pole from shoulder to shoulder
on which a dead cat was hung by a string, and the missionary said, " There goes a supper." No telling where the
cat came from—probably out of the gutter. No telling of
what it had died. But it had once lived, and therefore it
could support life. This is not true of all parts of China,

but it was true there. Therefore, what must have been a beggar woman!

But one day one of our Bible women came and sat down by this woman's side and began to tell her about the living and true God—who was not a dragon—who had created this universe, and who loved mankind and who loved women. The poor beggar woman shook her head in blind and uncomprehending unbelief. Day after day the Bible woman came and told her more of the story, told her how this God had given His only Son, who was born of a woman and who loved womanhood and who died upon the cross for women as well as men, and who would save all who came to Him. Day after day she shook her head. But one day her mind opened the tiniest crack to let in the light of this vision, which she had to admit was glorious, if only it were true. And through that tiny aperture of hunger and faith the Lord Jesus slipped in and transformed the heart and the life of this beggar woman.

When she had heard the whole blessed story, she wanted to tell it to others, and so asked if she might come to the Bible Training School and learn to read this blessed Book so that she could tell it to others. With money supplied by Christian women in America, her living was provided for and her rice paid for in the Bible Training School until she had learned to read, and then she went out as a Bible woman herself. Later her husband was converted, and their home was changed to a Christian home and became a center of transforming power.

And now we are permitted to see the glorious fruitage of the Gospel in the Christian son and these Christian grandsons. But what of the picture that the smallest boy was holding for us to look at? It was the picture of the oldest grandson, who had recently received his Ph.D. degree from Columbia University. Think of it! From the lowest degradation to the highest Christian culture in the third generation. Away with a trust in evolution! What evolution could not accomplish in a hundred thousand years was here accomplished in a few by the Gospel of Christ.

Christianity often has had the effect of at least reforming heathenism, even when it steadfastly resisted conversion. Gandhi, not a Christian, has opposed some phases of the caste system. Dr. Ambedkar, lifted from the low state of an outcaste and given a modern education, even though he has not yet become a Christian, has seen that it is time for the outcastes to give up their devotion to the Hindu religion and choose something higher. Even Nehru, who professes no religion, is indebted for part of his fine culture to the Christianity with which he has come in contact. Even his political ideas of freedom came not from paganism but from Christianity.

Not believe in Christian missions! We are all the product of missions. The Gospel did not start in America. The Bible was not written here. Jesus never set foot in one of our States. We are in an " uttermost part of the earth," far removed from where the Gospel started. How did it get to us? When I asked this one night in a church in Indiana a small boy on the front seat who had followed me piped up, " The missionaries," and he was right. We speak of " third generation Christians " in the Orient. Well, what are we? Only thirty-third or forty-third generation Christians—not yet far out of heathenism. Let us be humble and grateful. The cross of Christ is stamped on everything good which we have. It is upon our houses, our barns, our stores, our stock, our schools, as well as our churches. It is marked in our sanitation and our transportation. It is upon our fellowships and our fun. How blessed to be a Christian in a Christ-built land.

The good seed has produced much good grain.

IV

THE CHURCH'S RESPONSIBILITY FOR THE DOMINANCE OF EVIL AND FOR THE PRESENT WAR

For the name of God is blasphemed among the Gentiles, because of you, even as it is written.—ROMANS 2: 24.

THIS word of Paul, quoted from Isaiah 52: 5, is even more applicable to the Christian Church than it was to the Jews. They had been " faithless in a very little," while the Christian Church has been " faithless in much." They had been a tragic failure in many ways in their little land. The Christian Church, judged by what it has had to work with, its opportunities and its powers, has been the most tragic, inexcusable and awful failure in all history. The name of God has been blasphemed in numberless instances because of what the Church has been. The name of God has continued to be blasphemed by fearful idolatries and horrible superstitions because of what the Church has not been and has not done.

We must face now some hard facts, and the sooner we face them the less hard it will be. Recall again that Dr. Henry Van Dyke said that it is better to believe the saddest truth than the merriest lie. We have believed in the past a great many very merry lies, and are in danger of believing more. Many are now indulging in the merry lie that if we can only win this war and put Germany, Italy, and Japan where they belong, where they can no longer attempt to enslave the world, a beautiful and well-nigh perfect civilization will blossom forth. But Professor Sorokin has insisted that

Hitler, Mussolini, and Stalin are not causes but results of the world decay. We have been believing the merry lie, taught us by some of those highest in authority in our land, that the expression which our Lord gave us, illimitable in its spiritual meaning, the " abundant life," means only social security, a full dinner pail, abundant leisure to play golf and to fish, a car for every member of the family, gasoline, oil, and rubber enough to keep it going, and other equipment for the ardent flesh.

One of the notable books of recent years with a very striking title is that by Margaret Slattery, *Thy Kingdom Come, But Not Now*. It is brilliantly written, and it shows the social inequalities of life; but one reading it must be forced to the conclusion that, with the author's plea for enough milk for the little child in the slums, and enough economic ability to destroy the slums, and with the little apartment and the automobile and dog for the young couple starting out in life, and with all similar desirable things, she has not, for one moment, envisaged the Kingdom of God, but simply the kingdom of man. It is a book without a soul and envisages society devoid of spiritual life.

Dr. Walter Horton, in 1939, delivered a sermon in Seattle on the theme, " The Church's Midnight Hour," of which he says: " At eleven A. M. on a Sunday in September, speaking at the People's Church, I saved civilization on paper just as it broke down in fact. . . . The fact is that civilization in the democratic nations is very badly disintegrated and cannot be saved without deep-going reconstruction, starting in a rediscovery of the Christian bases of democracy and involving every aspect of life from center to circumference." He is not indulging in any merry lie, and the Church must not.

The first thing for the Church today is to awaken to its tragic failure through the centuries to fulfill in any glorious and victorious way its mission of evangelizing and Christianizing the world.

It is now for us to look squarely and fearlessly at the fact that the Church is responsible, by her perversions and failures, for the evils which are dominant in the world and for this present devastating and increasingly awful war. Not all evil can be put down, but it can be restrained from being the dominant and destroying force it so often is.

I. THE CHURCH IS RESPONSIBLE FOR RELIGIOUS EVILS DOMINANT IN THE WORLD TODAY

The special field of the Church is religion. It was set to purify the spiritual life of the world from its putrid pollutions. But if the fountain becomes impure, how can its stream be pure? and how could an impure Church purify the foul streams of false religion? The fountain of Christian truth has become many times in the past fearfully infected and still is today.

In the second century the Church, made up largely of those who had been converted from heathenism, became infected with the essential vices of heathenism itself. It would be a fine thing, if people, when they are converted to Christianity, would leave out all elements foreign to its life. But such is not the case, even today, since people often come into the Church with gross superstitions and erroneous and fleshly philosophies clinging to them; and it was notably not so in the days following the apostles.

Heathenism is one of the two basic religions in the world, the other being Jewish and Christian monotheism. There are many varieties of each, but every form and phase of religion stems from one or the other of these two roots. Heathenism began in the Garden of Eden with an attempted salvation by works. That is its basic element. The first sinners sought to make themselves proper and protected in the presence of Deity, which is the province of religion, by their own efforts, and they lamentably failed. The true religion was also revealed in the Garden of Eden as salvation through the grace of God, who, in His love, *came* into the region where the sinners were, *called* them to Himself, *convicted* them of their sin, *condemned* them to disciplinary punishment, and then *covered* them, not simply with coats which He made from the skins of beasts which had been slain in their stead, but with His forgiving grace. Since that day there have been basically only these two religious principles in the world—the true and the false, salvation by grace and attempted salvation through works, through the acquiring of merit which the sinner does not have naturally.

However, some time after those earliest days there was added to heathenism the supposed magic of ceremonies which springs from the principle of " works " with the support of a false supernaturalism. Just when that came in, we do not know; but we find it very early. And from that day to this, one of the marks of heathenism has been the conviction that through certain ceremonies one is changed and made suitable for the heavenly Kingdom. In the Eleusinian mysteries and in the Delphic practices this is clearly revealed among the Greeks; and throughout the heathen world, as we know it today, there is the belief that ceremonies bring about essential changes. For that reason our missionaries have to be very careful not to baptize people until they know that they have been regenerated, for the heathen people are willing to add any number of ceremonies, if only they are not asked to change their lives.

This infiltration of heathenism began to enter the Church through Judaism; for man, in the pride of his heart, ever tries to save himself. Judaism, at the time of the Apostles, was almost essential heathenism, even when it professed faith in Christ, for it was trusting supremely in outward works and forms. The Apostle Paul hurled himself successfully against it, and the Epistle to the Galatians is the great broadside that essentially destroyed it as a church movement. Gnosticism also raised its head in those days—" that heresy from the hotbed of the dreamy East." John and Paul both fought it, and so long as the apostles lived, they sought to keep the Church measurably pure, by their controversy against error.

But no sooner were they dead than the errors of sacramentarianism appeared unopposed dominantly within the Church. Especially did the doctrine of baptismal regeneration come in like a flood. We find Justin, who was so great a Christian that he became a martyr, and has since carried the name " Justin Martyr," saying in one place, " This is the way we regenerate people. We take them down to the river and there we regenerate them." Imagine one of our non-liturgical pastors saying, as he baptized a person, " In the name of the Father, Son, and Holy Spirit, I now regenerate you." He would be subjected to a church trial right away. Tertullian, another great leader, says, " As the water puts out the fire in the tow soaked with pitch, so do the waters of baptism put out the fires of sin in the soul." Could there ever be a more palpable or dangerous error than that, teaching that water, instead of the Word and the blood of Christ, cleanses from sin? I have always tried to be careful in baptism, which is first a burial, not to bury anyone thus until there was good evidence that that person was dead— dead unto sin, dead to self, and alive to God, of which the rising again is a symbol. I have sought not to use the form until I was sure the person baptized had the fact. But no matter how careful we are, again and again we find that we have baptized people who are yet in their sins and very much alive to them; and only the most fanatical will say that the fires of sin were put out in their souls by the waters of baptism, even by total immersion.

This sacramentarianism, this claim that baptism and the Lord's Supper are powerful agents to change the recipients, is, I believe, a fulfillment of the word of Jesus that the case of the Kingdom of Heaven would be like having leaven hid in some meal until the meal was thoroughly damaged by the leaven.

In my first sermon in my first church I took for my text the parable of the leaven and gave the usual interpretation— that the leaven is the Gospel and the meal represents humanity, and that as the leaven works from particle to particle until all is leavened, so the Gospel will work from person to person until all are converted. But when I came to subject this passage to sound scientific exegesis, I saw that it would not bear that interpretation. Historical exegesis alone will set it aside, for we must take that word in the sense in which those who heard it would understand it. In those days leaven was always considered in religion to represent the principle of evil, since it was a ferment. Jesus warned His disciples to " beware of the leaven of the Pharisees and Sadducees." Paul writes to the Corinthians:

" Your glorying is not good. Know ye not that a little leaven leaveneth the whole lump? Purge out the old leaven, that ye may be a new lump, even as *ye are unleavened*. For our passover also hath been sacrificed, even Christ; wherefore let us keep the feast, not with old leaven, neither with the leaven of malice and wickedness, but with the unleavened bread of sincerity and truth " (I Cor. 5:6–8).

They had not been leavened but " unleavened " by the Gospel. There is no other place in the Bible where leaven could be understood in a good sense. Why should we think that it was so used here?

Then we must keep careful watch of our context, our logical exegesis. In the twelfth chapter we learn that the hardness of heart and blindness of the ruling classes of Israel had culminated in their charging Jesus with working His miracles through the power of Satan. He warns them that they are in danger of calling the Holy Spirit Satanic; and, if they get that far, there is no hope for them. He realizes that the opposition of the heart and mind of these rulers has reached its peak, and He makes a definite break with them at that time, never again seeking directly to save them. Judaism, He sees, is hopelessly infected with evil. Then, in the thirteenth chapter, Jesus looks ahead and describes what the Kingdom of God will suffer in the new age of the Church which He is introducing. Human nature among Christian people will be the same as it was among the Jewish people, and the work of God will be perverted. Every one of these parables in the 13th chapter of Matthew, except those of the " treasure " and the " pearl," reveals to us our Lord's perception of what His cause would suffer.

Now, what is the true picture of this parable of the leaven? I believe it is this: During the Passover time not only were they not allowed to use leavened bread, but they must have no leaven in the house. In those days it was not easy to get leaven. One could not go to the corner grocery and buy yeast cakes; neither could one send over to the neighbors', as our mothers used to send us, when we were children, to get some of the " emptyings," as the leaven for salt-rising bread was called. Why it was called that, I do not know. But I know it had an odor that caused me to hold my nose when I brought the pitcher full of it from the neighbors', and I longed to empty it out. The Gospel is surely not like that. Here was a Hebrew woman who had some leaven in the house. She did not want to waste it. She was very frugal. And so, watching when no one was around, she took it and surreptitiously (that is what the word " hid " means) thrust it into the big quantity (three measures—a bushel and a peck) of meal which she had, thinking that when the Passover season was over, she could get it out again and use it. But alas, when she went to get it, she found that it had caused moldiness to pass through the whole quantity.

At any rate, something exactly like that is what happened in the middle of the second century. Heathenism was surreptitiously injected into the Christian Church, so that no one perceived the evil which was being done; and from that it has spread throughout the entire Church and is permeating it to this very day. There were no fundamentalists at that time, as there had been in the Apostolic Church, to combat the error while they were proclaiming the truth.

How did this work evil? It fixed the mind upon a falsehood instead of upon a fact. It put a ceremony in place of Christ, a work of man instead of the work of God.

Furthermore, the corollary of baptismal regeneration, the teaching that one cannot be saved apart from baptism, is quite naturally infant baptism. No one wants an infant to be lost; therefore, if baptism is necessary to save it, it must be baptized. Therefore, the theory of infant baptism came in then as the legitimate child of the philosophy of baptismal regeneration. This is history and should be frankly faced. And yet infant baptism did not become universal until well into the sixth century. That was because of another error which was taught, showing what they considered to be the supreme efficacy of this " sacrament," namely, that the sins committed before baptism, original sin and the sins which appeared in life, were all washed away forever by baptism; while the sins one committed after baptism must be taken care of by personal prayers, penances, etc. Therefore, it became the universal habit to postpone baptism just as long as one dared before one died, so as to have one good big

spiritual washing of the soul before death, and thus one
would go into heaven measurably clean.

The first historic instance we have of anything other than
immersion as the mode of baptism was a procedure designed
to meet this need of baptism just before death. Novatian,
one of the great leaders of the Church, was taken desperately
ill, and they thought he was about to die. He had never
been baptized. It would be a terrible thing to have a leader
of the Church die and go to hell because he was not baptized. But what should they do? If they immersed him,
the very immersing might kill him, and they would not be
able to tell whether he died first or got baptized and thus
saved first, and they did not dare to take that risk, which
seemed a real one. So the expedient of pouring water all
about his couch was resorted to, thus symbolically covering
him with water. He recovered, but because he did not think
that this baptism was sufficient, he was later baptized by
immersion. But from this time on, we find an increasing
number of cases where some such form in lieu of immersion
was resorted to for persons about to die. Sometimes they
would have the patient put his head out over the couch, put
a little water on it, and then pour a little on his hands and
feet. Thus he was typically immersed. Cyprian then taught
that it was not the amount of water that counted, a little
would do for symbol as well as much; and thus sprinkling,
in these cases, was resorted to, but only where there was
imminent danger of death. Professor Payne of Bangor Theological Seminary (Congregational) said in 1878 that " anyone who contends that anything other than immersion was
the almost universal practice of the Christian Church for the
first twelve centuries betrays either utter ignorance or sec-
tarian blindness." At the Synod of Ravenna in 1311 it was
decreed by the Roman Catholic Church that from that time
baptism could be by immersion, pouring or sprinkling, the

theory of the Church being that since the Church produced the Bible it could change it.

But what harm did all this do—this teaching that baptism saved, this later induction into the church of the infants, and this change in the form of baptism? This is a fair question and should be fairly answered. At least, it had this effect: the Roman Catholic Church, with all her perversions, never could have existed had not the multitudes been swept unregenerate into the church through the ceremony of baptism; and the Greek Catholic Church, with all her perversions, never could have existed had not the unregenerate been swept into that body through baptism with the teaching that thus they were saved. Professor Latourette tells us that at some time about A. D. 500 almost the entire population were professing Christians and members of the church. Baptized in infancy, they were taught that they were saved because they belonged to Christ's Body, the Church. Here the foundation was laid for all of the corruptions which succeeding centuries have mourned. This laid the foundations for the corruption of the clergy. Dr. Walter Horton has well said, " The vices of the clergy deserve all the lashing they get. The spectacle of a John XXIII or an Alexander VI claiming to be the Vicegerent of God and receiving homage of deluded millions is enough to arouse the wrath of men and of God."

This evil doctrine of baptismal regeneration, with its teaching that infants apart from the water baptism are lost, has persisted to this day. In the Old Granary burying ground in Boston you will find, among the tombs of the colonial worthies, an " infants' tomb." When I asked the caretaker what that meant, he said, " This is the place where the Puritan fathers chucked in [those were his words] the babies that died without being baptized," supposing that they were lost and that therefore this particular tomb would have a straight passageway to perdition. I said to him that there was certainly need then of Baptists arising to teach plainly that baptism did not save. He replied, " There was certainly need for somebody to teach it." Farther down Tremont Street, at the King's Chapel burial ground, you will find another " infants' tomb " for the same purpose. I have been asked to baptize babies because their parents were afraid they would be eternally lost if they should die. This is a mark of heathenism. The Bible makes it plain that we are covered by the atonement of Jesus Christ until, by deliberately choosing sin and rejecting Him, we lose our part in His sacrifice. John says, " He is the propitiation for our sins, and not for ours only, but also for the sins of the whole world "; thus the world is potentially saved. Therefore, the babes and the little children who have not yet deliberately chosen sin and turned their backs upon the Lord are covered by the blood of His sacrifice and do not need the heathenish marks of magic.

Another great evil which has perverted the Church so largely entered in the middle of the fourth century with the union of Church and State. Constantine, who was an astute politician, perceiving the ten million professing Christians who were in the Roman realm at that time, and desiring to line them up on his side, professed to have seen in the sky the sign of the cross with the words in Latin, " By this sign, conquer." He therefore freed Christianity from the bondage it had been under by preceding emperors and made it one of the legitimate religions of the Roman Empire. This placed him at the head of the Church, and the Church unwisely welcomed it. He was never even baptized until just before his death. He urged the people to be baptized, and in 324 he is said to have promised to every convert to Christianity twenty pieces of gold and a white baptismal robe, and twelve thousand men, with women and children in proportion, were baptized in one year in Rome. The Church allowed him to preside at the council when the crucial dispute between Athanasius and Arius was being settled.

What is the evil in the union of Church and State? We might better ask, What evil cannot be traced to the union of Church and State? Someone has well said that there is scarcely a war which has cursed the western world that has not been linked up in some way with the union of Church and State. Not only did Gregory VII seek to bring civil authorities all under the power of the Church, but Luther and Zwingli sought to use the civil power of the princes to carry forward their reforms. What is the plight of Germany today? If the principle of the union of Church and State which Luther saddled upon the Germanic people is the true principle, then Hitler, the head of the government, is the head of the Church, and has the right to command it.

The Puritans in New England carried over that principle and set up their government here in America as an absolute union of Church and State. What would that have meant to America had not Roger Williams and the Quakers in the North and the Baptists of Virginia in the South early pitted their lives against this principle? And to this day we have to fight the encroachments of the Roman Catholic Church, which seeks again and again to break down this separation of Church and State. We also have had to fight Congress, which was proposing to put the churches into the Social Security Plan, whereby the State could put the padlock upon the door of the Church, if it did not conform to the law, and the State for a time made churches a collecting agency for the Victory tax. Whatever has the power to tax has the power to destroy. The " etiquette of the flag," as it has been enunciated from Washington, is causing a lie to be told each Lord's Day in most of the churches in America.

The flag, by being placed at the right of the pulpit in the place of pre-eminence during worship, with the Church flag put at the left, in the secondary place, is made to say that the nation is above the Kingdom of God, the President of more importance than Jehovah. This is not true and it is not Americanism. Our men are fighting for the " four freedoms," are they? Well, there can be no religious freedom if the State is above the Church, and that is what that arrangement of the flags is saying. In the navy the Church flag is run up above the Stars and Stripes during worship. Let us place the flags in the right, the American relationship in worship, or else quit singing, " Protect us by Thy might, great God, our King," and get ready for religious enslavement some day, as the people are enslaved in Russia and Germany.

Another evil in the religious life which the Church by her perversions has been responsible for is that of worldliness. Jesus said of His disciples, " They are not of the world, even as I am not of the world." How strange that language sounds in the presence of multitudes of professing Christians in our churches today, as well as in the case of the dominant rulers in many a church period! How like a flood worldliness swept into the Church when its threshold was lowered! And what a fearful story of corruption ecclesiastical history often is, not only that of the Roman Catholic Church, but also that of the Church of England, from which because of its sins the Puritans had to break away. John Lord, in his *Beacon Lights of History*, treating of Papal evils, after speaking of the glory and grandeur of Rome, says:

" And yet of what crimes and abominations has not the government of the Church been accused? . . . What wars has not this Church encouraged, what discords has she not incited, what superstitions has she not endorsed, what pride has she not arrogated, what cruelties has she not indicated, what countries has she not robbed, what hardships has she not imposed, what deceptions has she not used, what avenues of thought has she not guarded with a flaming sword, what truth has she not perverted, what goodness has she not mocked and persecuted? Ah, interrogate the Albigenses, the Waldenses, the shades of Jerome of Prague, of Huss, of Savonarola, of Cranmer, of Cloigny, of Galileo; interrogate the martyrs of the Thirty Years War, and those who were slain by the dragonnades of Louis XIV, those who fell by the hand of Alva and Charles IX; go to Smithfield and Paris on St. Bartholomew; think of gunpowder plots and inquisitions, and Jesuit intrigues and Dominican tortures, of which history accuses the Papal Church —barbarities worse than those of savages, inflicted at the command of the ministers of the gospel of love! "

Nothing is weakening the Christian Church in the present day more than worldliness, not simply in the Roman Catholic Church, but throughout Protestantism, with here and there exceptions on the part of smaller bodies and of sound evangelical churches. So many of our churches are but religious clubs, and they do not differ essentially from the world, except in name. What power can they have? Why should the world give any attention to them? Why should it look for Christ within the Church any more than in the world, when the world is so dominant in the Church?

Back of all the other religious evils and the fertilizing father of them all is the evil of unsound teaching, of false doctrine, for doctrine is the source of life. We have seen the effect of the theological errors in the earlier life of the Church. They have been no less fruitful of evil in the later life. Reinhold Niebuhr, in his penetrating volume on *The Nature and Destiny of Man*, points out how liberal thinking, both philosophical and religious, since the days of the Renaissance has based its thinking upon the thesis of Plato, that human nature is naturally good, and that all that it needs therefore is education and culture; while both history and the Bible emphatically deny this, and prove that human nature is essentially evil and needs redemption. This teaching, together with the materialistic philosophy of evolution, has so denatured Christian teaching in vast areas, and especially in the schools, that civilization has been greatly speeded in its degeneration from a spiritually-centered civilization to the " sensate civilization " which Professor Sorokin declares to be dominant to the very destruction of civilization today. The unitarianism which gained such a foothold in New England in the beginning of the nineteenth century and the unitarianism which masks itself under the name of modernism today have that same anti-Biblical and anti-Christian thesis, that human nature needs only culture and not conversion. This cuts the nerve of evangelism and of missions, the two great energies of the Christian Church; and it prevails so largely in our modern Christian thought that there has been paralysis instead of power in these regenerative forces for the world.

II. THE CHURCH BY HER PERVERSIONS HAS BEEN RESPONSIBLE FOR VAST NATIONAL EVILS

Where there was union of Church and State the king became head of the Church and therefore the Church became in part responsible for the government's actions. Think of the perversion of the Gospel in Russia and the vast political eruptions which were caused by it. Think of Philip II of Spain, and of the Duke of Alva flooding Holland with the blood of the faithful! Think of Spain and her conquests, which were always made in the name of the Church! A recent book, describing Columbus on his third voyage made under the blessing of the Church, tells how the seamen ravished the simple and innocent natives whom they found in the Caribbean Islands and killed those who resisted.

Cortez conquering Mexico, Pizarro crushing Peru, all in the name of the State which was also the Church, not only wrought revolting cruelties, but laid the foundations for the baptized paganism which afflicts Mexico and South America today. I am praying daily for the Allied nations to win in this present war for freedom, and yet we know that the sins of all these nations have been many. The East India Tea Company was given power to keep the missionaries out of India, and they tried to keep them out of China. Sir John Bowring, who wrote *In the Cross of Christ I Glory*, did all he could as consul at Canton to keep the missionaries out of China. The " opium wars " cannot be forgotten. I do not approve of India's seeking at this time, or at any other time, simply to drive England out of India. I believe that the evils which would result from sudden independence would be far more than the evils under which the people of India now live, and yet I am convinced that if England had sought to elevate the masses of India by making them literate, and economically free by letting them manufacture their raw materials in their own land, there would be a different story to tell today. And in England, with the union of Church and State, and with the King as the head of the Church, the Church is involved in whatever England does politically. Had Gandhi not found in South Africa serious race discrimination fostered by government, and had he found a Church less coldly formal and more evangelistic and filled with the love of Christ, how different history might have been.

In America the Puritans' treatment of the Indians, and later the slave trade, which was sanctioned by the Church, show how easy it has been for the Christian Church, perverted by evil, to take sides with evil in national government. This story of the Church being party to its evils through her false alliance with government could be continued indefinitely. Had Christian people protested the Oriental Exclusion Act, as they ought to have done, there would have been one less cause for our present war.

III. THE CHURCH IS RESPONSIBLE FOR SOCIAL EVILS IN THE WORLD

We are not only responsible for what we do, but for what we might do. Since the Church was endowed with power to be salt and light, since the Church has the power of the Holy Spirit, wherever it has attained political power or the power to shape the life of a community it has been responsible for what evils it has permitted to thrive. Former Ambassador Bryce said sometime before he died that the white race had never touched in a commercial way any other race in the world without debasing it. What a devastating indictment that is, but how true it has been historically! And yet these sailors and merchants of the white race who went out to enrich themselves and at the same time further debased the heathen peoples by their covetousness and corruption, all doubtless professed to be Christians and would certainly have said with vehemence that they were not heathen.

We need not go back over the ancient history of the Church to prove the Church's guilt along this line. Take our own land and our own times. Here is the vast evil of strong drink. Prohibition was finally carried, to the great blessing of America, by an aroused Church; and then, when it was put upon the statute book, the Church went into hibernation. The enforcement of the prohibition laws was vested in the Treasury Department, whose head was Andrew Mellon, a church member who himself had been a large owner of distillery stock. What interest did he have in the enforcement? The President, a church member and a Baptist, let the White House and the District of Columbia be the scene of constant and open violation of the law. Had the enforcement of the law been lodged with the Department of Justice, I think we would have had a different story. But, even so, had the Church remained as alive to the evils of lax enforcement as she should have been this could have been corrected.

Then came the propaganda of lies circulated by the liquor interests, and the Church people in great numbers weakly believed them. President Hoover, a professing Christian, appointed a commission, on which all members were professing Christians, to examine the effectiveness of " our noble experiment." They seemed to confine their survey to the large cities where bootlegging was carried on. They seemed to pay no heed to those vast stretches of country where youth had grown up without ever having seen a drunken person or having known anything at all of the effects of alcohol. They did not poll our colleges to find out, as the brewers already knew and so stated after repeal, that " during the prohibition days students had ceased to be beer conscious." Repeal was carried through in the somnambulism of the Christian Church. It was won by less than twenty-five per cent of the vote of the electorate. Only one State in the Union proved that an aroused Christian Church could head off repeal. All glory to South Carolina!

Multitudes of our churches today want nothing said against the liquor evil, lest it tread on the toes of some of their members. In one northern city of 150,000 there were, a few years ago, but three pastors who dared to speak for the W. C. T. U. The pastor of one of the large churches promised the session when he came that he would have nothing to say on the subject of liquor. The pastorate of the Methodist church suffered frequent changes because each pastor persisted in speaking against alcohol. The pastor in the Baptist church in this city was asked by official members to say nothing about this evil, but he persisted, and alienated the beer drinking element of his church. When the first World War broke out, we had a prohibitionist as Secretary of the Navy, and he dried up the Navy. We had in General Pershing one who had the clear vision and courage to say:

" Banish the entire liquor industry from the United States; close every saloon and brewery; suppress drinking by severe punishment to the drinker . . . and the nation will find itself amazed at its efficiency. . . . I shall not go slow on prohibition, for I know what is the greatest foe to my men, greater even than the bullets of the enemy."

Where is a General Pershing for us today? The Church indeed is raising its voice against the evils attendant upon the easy means for dissipation in the war camps; but, from the President down, how many of the members of the Christian Church are there who propose that the curses pronounced by God against the nation that encourages and profits by drunkenness, and the curse which naturally comes from the drinking evil, shall not fall upon us?

What stand is being taken systematically against the gambling evil, which is growing with fearful rapidity, and now is being proposed for the national government? Church people are helping to keep the card games popular and churches are making money by gambling games. Bank nights in the movies, which are a form of lottery, are patronized by church people; and this seems to be sweeping on unhindered.

A vast amount of the fifteen-billion-dollar crime bill of our country could be eliminated were Christian people wisely allied with the forces elected to put down crime. The movies and the so-called comic sections of our newspapers are the greatest schools of crime which have ever been known, and these can go on with their crime-making business because Christian people support them and do not protest against them. A weekday Bible school was established in one of the districts of our city which had been noted for its production of juvenile criminals. Some time afterwards the judge of the juvenile court stated that juvenile crime had been reduced fifty per cent since the weekday Bible school had been started there. The Church is not the spiritual or the social power that it should be in the lands where it has become dominant. We shall see later what can be done.

IV.   THE CHURCH IS RESPONSIBLE FOR THE WORLD DARKNESS WHICH STILL PREVAILS

Impurities have paralyzed the missionary power of the Church in days gone by. Nestorianism moved to the East, but it went with an emasculated message. Twice it penetrated China, in the seventh and thirteenth centuries; but it sought to make its way by eliminating what the rulers did not like, and therefore it made no permanent stand. Christianity was introduced into India, probably by the Apostle Thomas; but it failed to continue as an evangelizing force. Christianity failed to convert Ishmael, and therefore throughout the Arabian world there flared up the blighting curse of Mohammedanism.

Not only was the Church paralyzed in her power by impurities through much of the early period, but the reformers failed to reach out to spread the Gospel; and this was at a time when the Orient was entirely open. Roman Catholics were the only ones, through the Reformation period, who seemed to have a missionary vision. At that time they organized the Society of Jesus, the military missionary organization of the Jesuits, with Loyola as the commander-in-chief. Their men were sent to America. One of our large midwestern cities has her principal streets named for these missionaries. Francis Xavier was sent to the East, which he found open, as Marco Polo had found it. He went unhindered through India and into Japan, and came back with the report that he had baptized a million converts. His work, we knew, was utterly inadequate and superficial, though he gave much time to instruction. He told the people something about Jesus, more about Mary, gave them the Ten Commandments, and told them that if they would be baptized in the name of Jesus they would be saved. As we have said, the Orientals are always willing to take on more ceremonies; and when he asked how many were willing to be baptized, multitudes responded.

And yet, so permanent was some of his work, in Japan, though the government took action and placed a severe ban against the Christian faith, condemning all to death who would not stamp upon and spit upon a cross placed upon the ground, that, after two centuries, when finally the ban was lifted in 1858, it was found that there were many thousands who still claimed to believe in the name of Christ. Can we imagine what the result would be today had the Reformers sent missionaries with the true Gospel into that land to plant there the seeds of the Truth?

Then followed the Renaissance, the revival of learning, the vast expansion of secular civilization, and with it the movements of the merchants to circumnavigate the globe and trade with the peoples of the earth. But they took with them their vices, which so corrupted the people that the Oriental nations had the sense to shut their doors against them. The world conquests of the West, carried on by covetousness, were responsible for the shut and bolted doors in the East which later our missionaries encountered.

But before the missionaries went forth there was the crippling of the Church by Calvinism, which was carried to such extremes that the Church waited for God to save men, instead of going forth in obedience to His command. When young William Carey rose in a Baptist association and said that he felt some movement should be made for the salvation of the heathen, the Moderator, who himself had baptized young Carey, rose swiftly and said in a thunderous voice, " Young man, sit down. When God Almighty gets ready to save the heathen, He'll save them without any of your help or mine." Never did the devil get into the mouth of man a more terrible or devastating lie, for God had so arranged it that He could not save the heathen without the help of His people, and that help they were not giving. Finally, this cast-iron constraint was cracked, and Carey was sent out by a few brethren to begin the great era of modern missions.

But the especially tragic thing for us is that the evangelical churches in America and in England did not awake for the harvest which God was rapidly preparing for them. It was a sad fact that when the missionaries went out at the beginning of the 19th century, they found the doors in the East still closed. But it was not long before God began gradually to open them, and they were opened much more rapidly than He could open Christian hearts to pour out the help for which the heathen world hungered. During the past fifty years there have been open doors everywhere, doors off their hinges, and, more than that, millions of people pouring forth with eager hands reaching out for something that was better than they knew. Japan could have been evangelized in the 1880's. The missionaries of all the evangelical denominations were reporting that a kindly attitude on the part of the government and the people was manifested everywhere, that there was an eagerness for hearing the Word, that the great opportunity had come to spread the Gospel over Japan, not simply by missionaries, but by the Japanese themselves. Such a great voice as that of

Kanimori, with his three-hour sermon, was heard up and down the country. That voice, alas! was silenced for twenty-five years because of the infection of modernism from Germany, but recovered its clear tones later and again sounded forth. Our missionaries were frantically appealing for reinforcements to be sent out. Had we flooded Japan at that time with the Scriptures, with Christian schools, with the Gospel in all the rural places, so that now there would be several million converts, instead of a pitiable half million, the story of Japan would have been far different. By this time there would have been many followers of Jesus in high authority, and the military party would never have had the opportunity it has had in recent years to arise.

Dr. Stuart Nye Hutchinson, retiring moderator of the Presbyterian General Assembly, said upon retiring from office recently, as reported by *News Week:*

" Over a half century ago Guide Verbeck [noted Dutch-American missionary to Japan] came home from Japan and pleaded with the church in America. He told us that the door to Japan was open, and that we could take that island empire for Christ. He pleaded in vain. . . . Now we are giving thousands of our finest young men and spending untold billions of dollars to keep Japanese paganism from destroying our civilization."

That military party, indeed, was born of the militarism of Germany, which grew up in Germany because of the teaching of evolution and the failure of evangelical Christianity to permeate thoroughly that land. It found ready soil in Japan. Had there not been the first World War, there would not now be the second. And the failure of a Christian Church to evangelize the world completely left the way open for the rank weeds of wickedness to smother the true grain. The tares grew more rapidly than the wheat.

Communism swept over China because of the deep longing

for something better than they had. If communism is the political carrion that many think it is, let us remember that people do not eat carrion until they are starving. Why did not the Church give them the true bread and water of life?

We forget the situation in Europe during the past fifty years. The evangelical missions of the various denominations were thriving remarkably, even with the little backing which they had. There has been, for the past generation, a cry for evangelical seminaries in Europe. Young men were being converted by the Gospel, and had we furnished adequate opportunity for training them, they would have evangelized their own lands. The Methodists and Congregationalists have had extensive work in Europe which ought to have been supported to a far greater degree than it was. Northern Baptists in northern Europe and Southern Baptists in southern Europe have found the people ready for the Gospel; but there has been a pitiably small number of native people trained to give them the Gospel. Had this work of the evangelical faith been pushed in Europe, as it might have been during the past fifty years, we would have a different story to tell about that land. Who knows that the boy Adolph Hitler himself might not have been brought under the power of the Gospel, and thus the present war have been averted.

Over the earth there has been in recent years a whitening harvest for Christian reapers. In fact, we have been living *at the harvest time of all the ages.*

The fact that three-quarters of the world's population of two billion are in utter religious darkness, a billion of them never having heard of the death of the Saviour for them; and the fact that the most of these in comparatively recent years have been accessible to us and have been wonderfully receptive to the Gospel, when it has been preached in loving persistence, stand before the Christian Church as a fearful indictment of her selfishness and stupidity, her slumber, drugged by the opiates of the world in the face of the cry that the harvest time has come. This vast World War would never have rolled like a dark cloud upon us had the Church been all out for God, as now we are having to be all out for war. It is necessary now to blast Japanese transports and airplanes and send thousands to death; but while we are cheering the success of our armed forces in the various sectors of the war, let us remember that thousands of these are Japanese who ought to have been saved and made Christians by a Church on fire, as was the Early Church.

There is no escaping this blasting indictment that the world is in its present condition because of the sins, the failures, the perversions, the neglect of the Christian Church—because the salt lost its savor and the light was hidden under a thousand bushels. Our Lord said plainly that if the salt should lose its savor, it would be cast forth and trodden under foot of men. This is happening in our own land. The most terrible thing about the situation of the Church is that it is so completely ignored by the world. It is no longer considered a clinic for the deadly spiritual disease of sin for which the Church alone has the cure. People pass it by or run over it with neglect. Never in the history of Christianity was there a greater call for revival, a more urgent need for the Church to be all out for God and for a lost world. And never before have the " iniquities " of the Church so testified against it. We cannot escape the clear responsibility for the fact that evil is riding high today. We cannot say other than that God is sending this scourging. He is using the nations as of old to chastise this people for their sins. The war would not be upon us had the Church remained in the purity and power of her original purpose.

V

THE CHURCH COULD STILL CHANGE WORLD CONDITIONS

If my people, which are called by my name, shall humble themselves, and pray, and seek my face, and turn from their wicked ways; then will I hear from heaven, and will forgive their sin, and will heal their land.—II CHRON. 7:14.

LET us recall the texts with which we begin: " God sent his Son into the world that the world through him might be saved " (John 3: 17), and " As the Father sent me, even so send I you " (John 20: 21), and the Great Commission, as finally given to the disciples before our Lord ascended, " Ye shall receive power, after that the Holy Ghost is come upon you, and ye shall be my witnesses both in Jerusalem and all Judea and Samaria and unto the uttermost part of the earth " (Acts 1: 8). With these in mind, let us now focus our attention on the great statement in II Chronicles and see in it an assurance of God to His people that is as timely as it ever was in the history of the world.

With a great prayer Solomon had dedicated the Temple which he had built. Reciting before God the needs of his people and their need of God, and especially the need of forgiveness, he says as he comes toward the close:

" If they sin against thee (for there is no man that sinneth not); and thou be angry with them, and deliver them over before their enemy . . . if they return unto thee with all their heart and with all their soul . . . then hear thou from heaven, even from thy dwelling place, their prayer and their supplications, and maintain their cause, and forgive thy people which have sinned against thee."

That night, after the great dedication services were completed, we read:

" And the Lord appeared to Solomon by night, and said unto him, I have heard thy prayer. . . . If my people, which are called by my name, shall humble themselves, and pray, and seek my face, and turn from their wicked ways; then will I hear from heaven, and will forgive their sin, and will heal their land."

There never was a land that needed healing more than the land occupied by the nations that have been overrun by the aggressor, or the nations that are striving for the freedom of the world. The greatest healing ever conceived is that which is now desperately needed and will be needed more crucially before this war is over and after.

A retired pastor in the East writes:

" I am preaching in many churches, and all churches that I have contacted are icebergs spiritually, gone over largely to ritual and ceremony. There is manifest no fervor; the effort seems to be to produce an esthetic effect. No one's conscience is ever disturbed; there is no concern about the ' lost.' "

Leslie Weatherhead, writing in *The Christian Century*, says:

" Britain is—with the exception of a very small minority, mostly within the churches who have the real Christian outlook and experience—humanist to the core. . . . There is no sign anywhere of a religious revival. . . . Most churches are empty and most Christians disheartened. If peace came tomorrow most people would slip back into the old grooves. . . . It is probable that even the newly awakened social conscience would go to sleep again." *

This is a fearful indictment from one who knows.

But here stands the promise of healing. It has never been

* Quoted by permission of *The Christian Century*.

cancelled. Jehovah God does not say that if the *Hebrew* people shall humble themselves, pray, and seek His face and turn from their wicked ways, then He will heal their land. He made His gracious promise in the sweeping, general terms of " *My* people," whoever they are and wherever they are, His people responsible for the government of whatever land in which they may live, His people with power to serve Him, if only they will. God is the same throughout the centuries and the dispensations. His people are all equally precious to Him. His deliverance is ready for them upon His terms.

The Outreach and the Inreach of This Promise

First, observe in detail the four things which God expects from His people (they are inflexible), and then the three things which He assures them He will do (they are a certain conclusion of the conditions). At the outset they are to humble themselves. This does not mean an outward pageantry of humiliation, not the sackcloth and ashes which might be put on hypocritically, but the broken and the contrite heart, which is always a sacrifice acceptable to God and which is the beginning of the approach to God.

All that is needed to humble any of us is to see ourselves in the presence of God. The legend says that the peacock, which was strutting with tail feathers spread as a banner in brilliant array, looked down at his feet and was so ashamed of their crudeness and ugliness that his gorgeous tail feathers, of which he was so proud, suddenly dropped. When Isaiah saw himself in the presence of the Holy God, he was humbled to the point where he thought he was dying. Saul of Tarsus was humbled when he found himself in the blaze above the brightness of the sun which revealed to him the Lord Jesus. Humbling comes automatically to those who see themselves and their work, their sins, their failures, even their supposed goodness and glory in the light of what they ought to be, in the presence of the standard of God. Let the Church in America and in England and the other countries of Europe see itself in the mirror of Christ's perfection and it will fall on its face. Let it look at its course in the past and the present, as it will stand forth under the searchlight of the Day of Judgment, and it will prostrate itself in agony and fear before God, who is a Consuming Fire; then renewal of life will have come to the first preparatory stage. Confession of sin is almost a lost art of the soul. It must be revived. It will be when sin is poignantly felt.

Then, let men pray, pray from the depths to which their humbling will take them, saying with the Psalmist, " Out of the depths I cry to thee, O God." Prayer in the last analysis is the expression of desperate need,—need which can be met from no other source. The Greek word *deomai*, which is the basic word for the act of praying, means, first of all, to be in want of, to feel the need of, to be utterly devoid of; and it is in this sense that men must come to God to pray for mercy and power. Not only is man's extremity God's opportunity, but it is God's only opportunity. So long as man feels self-sufficient, he does not take hold upon God.

How long shall men pray? Until they have sought and found His face. Like the disobedient child, from whom the mother has averted her face, we must pray until that face turns radiantly to receive us. Brother Lawrence in the monastery " practiced the presence of God." That is strangely and tragically lacking in the religiosity which so often passes for religion of the Church today, which goes through its " service of divine worship " and too often goes out unchanged. Henry Drummond declared that one minute spent actually in the presence of Jesus Christ in the morning would change the whole day. Let us say to God as did the Psalmist, " When thou saidst, Seek ye my face, my heart said, Thy face, O Lord, will I seek." Much of the business of the Church is done in the presence of efficiency ideals, of political shrewdness, of the confidence of might and power, rather than in God's Spirit.

Jesus was lost by Mary and Joseph in the temple. Alas, in many a temple dedicated to worship, He is lost today. There is that picture of great power called " The Presence." You are looking in from the rear upon a great cathedral. In the chancel there is the blaze of light as the liturgy and the theatricals of formal worship are being carried on. But dimly, in the foreground of the picture, which is the section near the entrance farthest removed from the chancel, is Jesus Christ, standing by the side of a humble woman who is kneeling and praying. The artist seems to be saying that Christ may not be at all in the pageantry of worship, but He is certainly with the penitent. He will be with a genuinely penitent Church, but it must be poignantly penitent as the tragic situation of sin and neglect calls for.

And then the culmination of God's call is to turn from wicked ways. Alas, alas! What a plowing up and overturning of much of society itself this would call for. Mighty house-cleanings marked the days of the good kings of Judah, but they would be as nothing compared to what would be in the Western world if the people of God should undertake to cast out from their lives their churches, their social relationships, and their habits, all the things which offend God. What a turning there would be from the wickedness of worldliness in many forms—the wickedness of hypocrisies, the wickedness of fleshly and dispositional sins, the wickedness of unrighteous relationships among men; the wickedness of neglect of the things of God, of the profaning His day, of compromise, of conformity to the spirit of the age and the fashions of the world, instead of conformity to His will. The world would certainly know that something had hap-

pened if it saw the people of God universally convicted of
their sins and turning abruptly and totally from every way
of wickedness. Do these people dare to pray the prayer of
the Psalmist, who was so impressed by the omnipresence of
God that he exclaimed, " Search me, O God, and know my
heart: try me and know my thoughts: and see if there be
any wicked way in me, and lead me in the way everlasting " ?

Such a turning to God as this would mean something to
God. Heaven is not so far away that He would not hear.
The throne of God is not so occupied with the affairs of
the universe that it would not give attention. In fact, it
is so occupied with world affairs that it is listening in-
tently for such prayer with such accompaniment, and God
assures us He will hear in heaven. God says: " For thus
saith the high and lofty One that inhabiteth eternity, whose
name is Holy; I dwell in the high and holy places, with
him also that is of a contrite and humble spirit, to revive
the spirit of the humble, and to revive the heart of the contrite ones " (Isaiah 57: 15).

Let this be done and then from His throne of righteousness, justice, and truth, would go forth a mighty edict of
forgiveness. It would flow down like a healing stream over
the hearts of the humble, the broken, the penitent, the returning prodigals, the prodigal Church. The mightiest wave
of forgiveness the world has ever known would flow forth
from heaven. The scientists tell us of cosmic rays that have
strange effects on the earth, but this is the one great cosmic
ray that is needed to re-create the Church of God. Think
of what it would mean to have a forgiven Church, for
preachers and pastors to be forgiven the multitude of their
sins, their formality, their carnality, their vogue of being
men-pleasers, their self-seeking. Even the great business
magazine *Fortune*, in its editorial " The Light That Failed,"
has brought a terrific indictment against a Church which

has forced its pastors to preach what pleases men, and against pastors who have let themselves be thus manipulated until there is no clear voice, no prophetic word any more that is gripping and arresting and compelling. What a mighty blessing to have church officers forgiven, for the sins of many have been mountainous. And then think of the Church, the Body of Christ, the " continuation of the Incarnation," the visible representative of God upon earth— what would it not mean for it to be forgiven of all of its caricature of Christ, its misrepresentation of His ministry, its cancerous calumny of His character, its slumber and lethargy, when He is crying to it through the voice of history and of the present situation to lift up its eyes and look upon the fields that are white unto harvest the world around? What would it not mean to have the Church forgiven again, restored to His presence, and sent forth freshly anointed with His power?

The outcome of the present war will be one of two things: either the United Nations struggling for freedom will be defeated (though it does not now appear they will be) and thus be enslaved with such an awful, black, terrible slavery that Christ will be compelled to come to take His people out of the world, or they will win and, after a while, the Church will be given another opportunity to evangelize the world. But will it accept that opportunity? In all the discussion of the post-war conditions and plans, why is it that so little is said about a vast reformation of the Church and of an arousing of it to be all out for God and for the evangelization of the world? This kind of revival that we are talking about must come, or else the Church will further subject herself to the judgment of God. It is to be literally either revival or ruin.

But given such a returning of the Church to God in humbleness and prayer, and such a seeking of His face and a turning from every wicked way, God assures us not only that He will forgive His Church, but that He will heal our land. *This is America's only hope.* We can sing " God Bless America " until we are black in the face, but God is not going to bless America unless America repents. We can make fine plans for the balance of power in American society, but it will be just as futile as have been the attempts to balance political powers in Europe. Only God can save America, and He can save it only through His revived Church. Let that revival come this year, and the whole face of the war will be changed. God has not forgotten how to break the power of tyrants and dictators. We are told that Queen Elizabeth prayed and called upon all of her people to fast and pray when her navy, under Drake, went out to meet the Spanish Armada that was coming to overwhelm the land. God acted, and that terrific storm at sea broke the power of the invading host. If our trust is in our armies, our navies, our air force, we are doomed, even if we win. A pastor in Nebraska recently said that what we are really singing is " Pass the Lord and praise the ammunition." If our trust is in God, and if we put ourselves where we can trust in Him, there can still be hope for the world.

Vice-President Wallace, in an interview with Frank S. Mead of the *Christian Herald*, says: " If we are to have a decent peace and a decent world after the peace, two things must happen. Religion must expand and take in a lot more territory; and we must have a tremendous revival of the missionary crusade. It doesn't make much difference what else we do, unless we do this." And David Lawrence, in an editorial in the *United States News*, declares:

" We can shorten this war if we reach to the hearts of peoples, if we appeal to their consciences and their innate sense of fairness. We give lip service to the philosophy of Christ, but when it touches our pocketbooks, our trade, our positions of political power or pride, we forget those teachings. What we need is a militant Christianity and the courage to live up to it and make sacrifices."

Specifically, there are a number of things that the Church in this age can do.

The Church Can Promote Good Government

We are taking first what may be considered the ultimate fruit of the Gospel in human society. When the Church numbers among its membership a majority of the population, or even a strong minority, it is unquestionably in a position, if it will, to promote good government. And if it does not, whose is the blame? "To him who knoweth to do good and doeth it not, to him it is SIN" (James 4: 17).

Thus it becomes a sacred duty for Christian people, not necessarily for the Church as an organization, but for the people who form the Church, to see to it that right laws are passed and right men are placed in office to execute those laws. Someone has said that a democracy is just as good or bad as the people want it to be, and where the democracy is so largely dominated by church members, then our democracy is just as good or *just as bad as the church members want it to be*. We left our vacation one year and drove 230 miles, coming home sooner than we otherwise would have come, merely to vote at the primary election. We live in what is considered, in many ways, the best ward of the city. I think there are, however, more slackers in that ward, when it comes to voting, than in any other ward. At the last election in Chicago the notorious Kelly-Nash machine went back into power with but 116,000 majority, while a half million voters had not been to the polls. Christian people must stand at last and be judged before Almighty God for the way they have used or have failed to use the right of suffrage. This is no place to go into all the elements of sound government, but the conscience of the Church does need to be aroused to its responsibility to vote for men and for issues rather than in political slavery to vote merely for parties. There are both righteousness and rascality in all the parties, and it is the busniess of God's children to exalt the one and defeat the other.

The Church Can Promote International and Interracial Good Will

After building up sound and righteous government in its own land, a dominant church in any land should see to it that its nation's relations to other nations rest not on the selfish basis of economics, but on the sound, human, and divine principle of good will. We are finding that the nations of the earth do constitute a family and that they are being drawn closer and closer together; and therefore all the principles which make family life blessed should be manifested in the family of the nations. The Christian brotherhood of the churches in the various countries should be a bond that ultimately affects all international questions. Argentina and Chile went a long way when they placed on the crest of the Andes the heroic statue of Christ, with the great inscription, " Surely shall these mountains crumble sooner than these nations shall again engage in strife." This feeling is found in the relations between Canada and the United States, between which, for over a century, with a frontier of five thousand miles, there has never been a gunboat on their common waters or a military fort and guard along their borders. England and America also have been coming to that same sort of good will and mutual trust.

Would that that spirit had been manifested toward defeated Germany on the part of France and England. I have been told that an article by H. G. Wells published in a magazine just before the war, an article in which he put the blame for the rise of Hitlerism upon England and France, because they did not extend one finger of help to Germany, but left her to wallow in her helplessness in her efforts to become a republic, caused the whole issue of that magazine to be suppressed. England was not willing to face the sad truth. America, indeed, let Mr. Dawes go to Germany to help her get on a sound financial basis, but that was a very meager help. Our return to China of the unused portion of the indemnity fund which she had sent to us following the Boxer uprising so warmed the heart of China and so bound her to us as a friend that her friendship even survived our excessive unfriendliness to her in the selling of scrap iron and oil to Japan during the early years of the Japan-China conflict.

In recent years, when we had that strange depression from over-production, when we were made sick because we had more than we could eat, and the government ordered wheat and cotton plowed under, corn burned, pigs killed and turned into fertilizer, and trainloads of products dumped into the rivers in order arbitrarily to bring up prices, we committed one of the greatest and most criminal acts of folly which a nation could possibly commit. Had this vast over-production been bought up by our government and then been shipped freely to the needy people of the world, how different would be the attitude of the world toward America today! Who knows but that this one act alone might have kept the dreadful war from ever coming to our shores?

Certainly the Christian conscience of America should have prevented the absolutely unnecessary and senseless Oriental Exclusion Act of 1924. According to the quota law, not more than 145 Japanese could have entered the country in any one year. Japan was so eager at that time to keep the good will of America that she would readily have made a gentlemen's agreement with us by which no passports should be issued to any of her people. But to please petty politicians in one narrow strip of our country the proud nation of Japan was slapped in the face, and at that time she doubled up her fist and said, "Some day Uncle Sam shall feel this in his face." We were in Japan in 1924 and found that the social earthquake which it had caused was far more prolonged and ultimately more deadly than was the physical earthquake, the effects of which were still visible on the wharves of Yokohama. Japan recovered from the shattering effects of the earthquake of 1923, but she did not recover from the wounds to her spirit caused by our unfriendly act. This I know from our visit to Japan and from contacts with her people since.

And now, with seventy thousand American-born citizens of Japanese racial ancestry suddenly denied the rights of the Constitution, we have been, I believe, sowing the dragon's teeth. For college-bred young men and women to be subjected to all the indignities which internment of the Japanese occasioned, in spite of the evident purpose on the part of the officers in charge of this move to go as carefully as possible—for people to be ruthlessly torn from their surroundings and their businesses is something that America will yet pay for a hundredfold. I am told by those who had first-hand contact with the FBI that members of that organization stated that this vast internment was not necessary, that the FBI was perfectly competent to find out and take care of all dangerous characters. But even granting that something special needed to be done, it is quite clear that the drastic action taken was due to race prejudice and covetousness on the part of a relatively small group of people on the Pacific Coast. Even before Pearl Harbor the situation was so bad that groups of Christian women in a certain section of California did not want a missionary who was doing a notable work among the Japanese to come and tell them about it!

Statements made in Lathrop Stoddard's book, *The Rising Tide of Color*, which appeared after the First World War, seem to be nearer than ever to fulfillment. A cultured Chinese in Harvard University told one of our laymen that he was convinced the next great war would be a war of the colored races against the white races. When cultured Negro preachers are physically assaulted for merely walking through a car in which white people are seated, as recently happened, we are getting very rapidly not only into a bad way but into the worst of ways. The Christian Church must promote rapidly international and interracial good will or it will itself be throttled in the strife which will arise. The Christians in Japan and China, praying for each other, point to an attitude which should prevail everywhere.

The Church Can Promote Social Righteousness

As we have said before, there is no such thing as a social gospel. Gospel is good news. Your duties are not good news; they are responsibilities. We should use words discerningly. But, on the other hand, neither is there any true Gospel of the Son of God which does not issue in social righteousness, which does not bear the fruits of justice and peace and good will among men. This we have too often forgotten. Jesus Christ does produce a Christian civilization when He gets the chance and has the consecrated cooperation of His people.

A great and a needed work was done during the past generation by those who insisted that men who claim to be Christians, who have been regenerated by the Holy Spirit, should show that they are new creatures and true Christians in their relationship to their fellow men. These apostles of social righteousness have often erred, and erred seriously, in thinking that there was some way in which society could be raised wholesale, without the need of waiting for men to be born again. The mistake has been that of trying to instill the ethics of Christianity into the pagans of society without first bringing the pagans to Christ to be made by Him into new creatures.

We can pass righteous laws. But, as the physical body moves in health and entirety by one part caring for all the others, so human society can be what it ought to be only when one member in it cares for and treats rightly every other member in it. Unquestionably there has been a vast amount of covetousness and cruelty passing apparently under the cover of Christianity, because professing Christian men have been guilty of these evils. Unquestionably a vast amount of callousness has gone into the relationship of the strong with the weak, and when these strong men profess to be Christian, Christianity gets the blame. In the town where I had my first church, however, we saw it work differently one year. The Cigar Makers' Union went on strike. They sought then to pull out every other union in a sympathetic strike. They were working pretty well, until they came to the men working for Mr. F——— in one of the great lumber mills. Mr. F——— was a leading Methodist layman and a Christian. Not all Methodists are Christians, any more than those in other denominations. But he was a Christian. When these labor leaders came and asked his men to go on a strike, they said: " No. Mr. F——— has always treated us as a Christian man should. He has always been fair. He has listened to every one of our complaints, and when something could be done, he has done it. And now we are not going to hurt him just to please you." The whole sympathetic strike broke at that point. On the other hand, I remember years ago going into a calcium carbide plant,

when this chemical was used widely for bicycle and automobile lights. The plant was full of fine dust. Many men
worked with sponges over their mouths. I asked the owner
of the mill, who was showing us through, whether this wasn't
pretty hard on the workers. He said, " Oh, no. It doesn't
hurt them." But I know that the Lord never intended
human lungs to breathe calcium carbide dust day after day.
I looked out upon the homes where his workmen lived. They
were anything but inviting. But up by the side of his
magnificent house on a hill was a great ravine, a vast chasm
which he, out of his profits, had turned into a veritable
paradise. I thought, as I contemplated the two scenes, how
much better in every way it would have been if he had filled
up the chasms in the lives of his employees, and had beauti-
fied their hearts and homes rather than pour into a mere
park the money which he had made by exploiting their toil.

Not only must social righteousness in industrial relations
be promoted, but the Christian Church must put down those
forms of iniquity which are a menace to the welfare of our
whole society. A few years ago twelve of our universities
appointed a commission to study twelve phases of the movie
business. It was one of the greatest surveys ever made.
When the facts were all in, the commission's work was
summed up in that remarkable book, *Our Movie-Made
Children*, by Henry James Forman. Seven great reviews of
this were published in *The Christian Century* by Fred East-
man. The commission had found that the movie business
as conducted was one of the greatest causes of nervousness
in children. It was the fruitful school of juvenile crime. It
was doing more than anything else to break down sex morals
and to break up homes. The commission summed up its
study by declaring that one of the mightiest educational
influences in the world was being conducted with less moral
regard for the welfare of the people than one would find in

voodooism of Africa. Why has the movie business been able to build up all its family-wrecking, soul-destroying, crime-producing influence? Because Christian people have patronized it in such numbers, swallowing down even the stuff which they do not approve of rather than unitedly serving notice that they would not patronize it at all until it became a pure stream in our social life. This, even without any laws, would have cleaned up the awful, putrefying, infectious mess.

The same is true of the liquor situation. Prohibition was finally carried by an aroused Church and aroused business Then both went to sleep. And while prohibition was a tremendous success, as has been proved by what has happened through repeal, Christian people believed the lies that were manufactured and peddled, and let repeal come in, as we have already observed, with less than a twenty-five per cent vote of the electorate. An aroused Church today could again secure prohibition, not simply for the Navy and the Army, but for the whole country. Why remain cringing citizens—slaves of the flamboyant lie-parading forces of alcohol?

Christian men and women, by uniting together, giving attention to it, and putting the right officials in power and then supporting them, can clean up the vast majority of social evils. That which in these days is being called " the social disease " could be vastly restrained if the Church would launch a campaign to call it by its real name, " the sinful disease," and to bring about the spiritual conditions and the aroused conscience which would again give us a measurably pure and decent society. Instead of that, remedies are being found for speedy cure in order that the lustful may go forward unchecked. Let men and women be led to cease from sin, and the " social diseases " would be effectually curbed.

The evils of the strife between capital and labor can be controlled by Christianity moving down into these regions in full force in the persons of the men who profess to be followers of Christ. The political follies of socialism and communism are not needed. The chairman of the deacons of one of our large city churches, one of the head men in a plant manufacturing parts greatly in demand, told me that his plant had never had a strike because, whenever trouble comes, the officials call the men in and they sit down together and look over all the facts involved. The men are satisfied with such arrangements as can be made, and so the work goes on.

America might as well face the fact that she is in for an industrial and economic revolution unless Christianity does what the Wesley revivals did in England. There are many pastors and laymen who think that what happens in politics and social relations is no business of the Church. But, since in a democracy like ours we are the political and social units, it is the business of all of us who profess the name of Christ to be Christian units through and through. One of the greatest evangelistic preachers of America is Dr. W. B. Riley, long of the First Baptist Church, Minneapolis. There was a continuous stream of converts under his ministry, but he did not neglect the social aspects of Christianity. One whole volume of sermons, *Messages for the Metropolis,* dealt with public questions in the days of a corrupt regime. Later, he with Dr. Dick, pastor of the Wesley Methodist Church, successfully, through public addresses and debates, fought to prevent the extension of the patrol limits for the saloons beyond a closely defined downtown area. True evangelism must ever be striking at the places of pollution of the souls of men and of society. Christianity can be salt and light today if it will, and if it won't, it will be steadily cast out and trodden under foot of men.

The Church Can Promote Revival

Revival indeed comes from God, and cannot be worked up by man. But it can be promoted in the God-given ways, as has been proved again and again. No great revival ever has blessed the world which was not born out of earnest prayer on the part of God's people, who discerned the vast need and who believed in God.

There has been in recent years a great reaction against revival. Many are afraid of the word. But it does seem strange to shiver with fear when that word is applied to the revival of religion. In business, revival is always welcomed, as it is in sports and in physical convalescence from sickness. This bad reaction began a generation ago. President George B. Cutten of Colgate University, in his remarkable book, *Instincts and Religion,** in speaking of modern theology, has this to say:

" In contrast to the appeals to the instincts which have been common in religion down through the ages, we have recently been experimenting with appeals to the intelligence—and not very successfully. Many of us can well remember with what great satisfaction and abounding optimism we welcomed the New Theology. Here was something logic-proof and entirely reasonable. No longer would men scoff at religion or laugh at its vagaries. We had finished forever with what we called emotionalism in religion and got down to a rock foundation. Very good! But what have been the results? Some people think that there is nothing colder than a dog's nose, but what about the New Theology? The truth is that the New Theology is dying on its feet because it is so purely rationalistic. It is too successful: it is a case of a cat drowning in cream. What we thought of as emotionalism, of which we were so shy, was really an appeal to the instincts, and frequently a very crude one. It carried emotion with it. . . .

" Worship programs have taken the place of devotional meetings, religious emphasis week has displaced the revival meeting,

* Harper and Brothers, 1940, pp. 87, 88.

and social betterment plans are substituted for celestial ambitions. These may be intellectually defensible but they are instinctively dull and unprofitable. . . .

"The unlettered minister on the rural hillside has no such inhibitions. He is not concerned with logic, and reason seems to obfuscate his style. His appeals to the instincts may be crude, but they are effective and permeated with motive power." *

This indicates that there is an awakening to the folly of the "safe and sane" evangelism which was launched to the disaster of the Christian Church. William Wistar Comfort, in his recent biography of Stephen Grellet, traces the work of this greatest of all Quaker missionaries during the days when the Romantic period, following the Deistic, had released men's emotions sufficiently so that they could get concerned about eternity, sin, and salvation. In those days "people were not ashamed to weep, either in the theater or in church"; but now a stoicism in intellectual and spiritual concerns has settled over the Church, so that more or less everywhere there is resentment when the emotions which produce action in life are stirred.

But love is an emotion, and the substitution of something intellectually mechanical, either in people's relationship to each other or in their relationship to God, is nothing less than suicide. Revivals in religion are perfectly normal and natural. A careful study of the universe shows that there is nothing which goes on in nature with absolutely even current. Not only are there the tides of the ocean and the seasons of the year, but it is known now that there is a pulse beat in plants as well as in animals. Revival means life again, new life, and access of life, after there has been a deficiency of it.

Revivals of religion are utterly Scriptural. Not only does the history of Israel and the Christian Church reveal that

* *Ibid.*, p. 89. Quoted by permission.

the true religion has gone forward by great pulsations, but there stand out in the past the great prayers which have brought this about. Peter speaks of " times of refreshing from the presence of the Lord." We read that there was joy in Samaria when a new sense of sin and a new discovery of God came to that city. What city in America does not need this form of refreshing! Years ago, in Minneapolis, J. Wilbur Chapman arranged with the churches to bring a number of evangelists to hold simultaneous meetings in various parts of the city. The city was swept by the love of God. Streetcars rang with the songs of joy and gladness. Conversions were marked everywhere. The whole city was permeated by the power of God. Nothing is so needed in Minneapolis today as the repetition of that experience.

Revivals are scientific. They offer the only way in which the Church can hold its own against business and pleasure and the schools. These institutions are continually having drives for increased life. It was not so long ago that the Church had vacant space, as it were, around her life. She had Saturday night, all day Sunday, and much time during the week. In my first church, our young people studying the Christian Culture Courses of the Baptist Young People's Union of America, which consisted of three great courses in the Scriptures, in missions, and in sacred literature, changed the meeting from Sunday night to Monday night, so that we could give an hour and a half to the three great lessons. Where could that be done today? The schools have pressed in, demanding all of the pupil's time. In some places the teachers actually and deliberately plan to control all of the spare time of the child out of school. Commencements are put on prayer meeting nights, without any conscience. No consideration is made for the church. Sunday study is the rule. On the other side, business has crowded in until churches all over the country are like Trinity Church in

Wall Street, New York, overshadowed, and looking as if it were almost crushed by the great commercial structures all about it. The business world has moved in to commercialize the Sabbath with the Sunday paper, placing before the people five times the amount of advertising that is given on other days. All Judas did was to make profit out of Jesus, and that is what the Sunday paper is doing, whether it realizes it or not, by carrying its commercialism into the Sabbath. Men are so driven with business that they have little time left for church activities.

And then in front and back of the Church is that maddening press of pleasure of every kind. The Church is literally having its life squeezed out by the encroachments of these great human agencies. Can this be changed? It must be changed. Or society itself will deteriorate further. When we think of the vast sweep which genuine revival would entail in private life and public life, in business, in amusements, in fashions, and in education we are staggered by the thought; but America faces either revival or ruin. It is our country's only hope.

The lack of the genuine and true spirit of revival has resulted in the promotion of Pentecostalism. Love must have warmth, instead of the atmosphere of the icebox. Formality is no fun. Vitality is vivacious. Let us admit that there are at times some excrescencies attending revivals of religion. Are there not similar excrescencies wherever there is a flood of life, all the way from the child jumping up and dancing and playing boisterously to the football and baseball fans yelling themselves hoarse, and business plunging wildly into speculation? Dr. John A. Earl, a number of years ago, in speaking for revivals, said that when he had rung the doorbell of a certain home, he could hear a sepulchral sound within the house. A prim woman came to the door and decorously admitted him. When he went into the living-room he perceived that everything was in perfect order, and he readily inferred that scarcely a piece of furniture had been moved for years. Why all this primness and preciseness? There were no children in the house. There was only decadent life there. From that place he went to another home. As he rang the doorbell, he heard the cries and shouts of children inside. Soon a woman came to the door, carrying a baby in her arm, with another child clinging to her skirts. She said cheerily, " Come in, Dr. Earl, if you can get in." And he went in. He stepped over one child on the floor. Very few things were in their proper place, but the house was full of life.

The question is, Which do you choose for the Christian Church—the abundant life of youth or the sterile, stereotyped life of senility? A vital young man from the middle West went East for some theological studies. He said that many of the churches of the East were well supported and had a dignified service Sunday morning. " Why," he said, " they have the same interest in keeping up the church that they have in keeping up the family burying ground! " Do they need revival? It would either " kill them " or bring them to life.

Another great proof of the soundness of revival is that it always starts among God's best people. It never starts with those who are far away from Him. It begins with those who love Him most, who begin to feel that, in spite of all their religious life, they are far away from Him and that their hearts are cold. They sing sadly, but with fulness of meaning, the hymn so tragically lacking from our recent hymnals:

> " Come, Holy Spirit, heavenly Dove,
>   With all Thy quickening powers,
> Kindle a flame of sacred love
>   In these cold hearts of ours.

" Look! how we grovel here below,
    Fond of these earthly toys;
Our souls can neither fly nor go
    To reach eternal joys.

" In vain we tune our formal songs;
    In vain we strive to rise;
Hosannas languish on our tongues,
    And our devotion dies.

" Dear Lord, and shall we ever live
    At this poor dying rate,
Our love so faint, so cold to Thee.
    And Thine to us so great?

" Come, Holy Spirit, heavenly Dove,
    With all Thy quickening powers;
Come, shed abroad a Savior's love,
    And that shall kindle ours."

The way revival begins and spreads is this: those who are really nearest to the Lord become aware of how far they actually are from Him, and they draw nearer. These are the best people in the church. Sometimes it begins, as it ought to, with the pastor, with the church officers. If not with them, then with some godly souls within the church. As these draw nearer to the Lord, then those who are a little further away become conscious of the widened space between them and God's best saints. They are convicted of sin, and repent and draw near to Christ. This makes the ones out on the fringe wake up to the fact that they are far away from the Lord and repentance and the desire to return begin to be manifested in them. When this has gone on sufficiently in the Church, so that it has separated itself in a widening chasm from the world, then, and not till then, does the world become convicted of its sin and we begin to find sinners converted. This is the natural, normal, scientific way in which revival spreads. Our Lord told His disciples, as recorded in the 16th chapter of John, " When he [the Holy Spirit] is come [that is, to the Church], he will reprove the world of sin and of righteousness, and of judgment to come." The Holy Spirit does not come upon the world first. He comes upon the Church. This is what happened on the Day of Pentecost. This is what has happened every day since, when people in the world have been convicted of sin. They have not been convicted except first some of God's people have been convicted of sin and have received afresh the Holy Spirit.

The heart's cry today is, To your knees, O Church of God. Humble yourself before Him. Pray. Seek His face until you find it. Turn from all your wicked ways. Let the world see that you are actually returning to God. Millions of souls will be saved, the Church will again be salt and light. Mighty things will happen in our land and throughout the earth.

The Church Must Promote Sound Teaching

The Church can and must proclaim sound doctrine if it is to have revival and life for its evangelistic and ethical tasks. The coldness of the new theology which Dr. Cutten deplored is not its greatest evil. It was cold because it was dead. It had denied the very truths which are the life of Christianity. Liberalism in religion has had a long enough time to prove its nature and power or lack of it, and it is the lack which has been proved. Evangelism and the services of prayer have dwindled and have disappeared under its blighting influence, as many have confessed. Many times in the history of the Church there has been a cold and sterile orthodoxy, but that has been because of spiritual decadence of the people; the truth has been there, but it has lacked life. But where truth as well as life has been lacking, the Church has made a sorry exhibition of paralysis of its vital functions.

For many years doctrine has been decried. It is a healthy and hopeful sign of returning sanity that quite generally it is being recognized that doctrine is the very soul of life. Next to prayer, the need for today is a reproclaiming with great conviction the basic, cardinal, fundamental dogmas of the Church of the supernatural (or superphysical, if you please) powers of God as manifested in the production of His Word, the Bible, as exhibited in the person and work of His Son, as shown in the regeneration wrought by the Holy Spirit. People are manifestly hungry today for a true, sincere, and earnest exposition of the great truths of sacred Scripture.

The philosophy of unproved and unprovable evolution has developed the poison of materialism until the soul of society is stagnated. There needs to be a great transfusion of the blood of Christ, for bloodless theologies have brought on a pernicious religious anæmia. T. R. Glover, before he left us, sent forth an alarm that those hymns exalting " the blood of the Lamb," which he says is " the central point of all history," have largely disappeared from our hymnals. For great revival there is needed great preaching, and great preaching is the proclamation of the great truths of God and of His redemption of us through His Son. Every great revival has come through the re-emphasis of great neglected truths. There has been a woeful decadence in the preaching which produced the victorious Church of former days. Men can eloquently ring the changes of the day and of social cures, but this can never take the place of preaching the great Word of redemption through the crucified and risen Son of God. The evangelists of the world have been the evangelists of the Word.

The Church Can Still Promote Missions

This is the main business for which the Church was launched. At the very close of each one of the Gospels, and at the beginning of Acts, is the record of the work that our Lord laid upon His disciples before He left the earth. It is in such brief terms that the one thing the disciples were to live for is easily overlooked. Carrying out the Great Commission, spreading the Gospel out from the Church to the ends of the earth, is not simply something that may be done in addition to all else that we do; it is *the one thing above all else that we are to live for*. The Great Commission draws a circle around the Christian life, and it says that there is to be nothing in your life which does not bear upon that great work. Why? Because it was for this that the Son of God came to the earth—that the world might be saved, that men everywhere might know the love of God. And before He went away, He said, " As the Father sent me, even so send I you." Everything in the life of the Son of God upon earth was made to bear upon the one thing of getting the Gospel known in the world.

Therefore, I must take the Great Commission as a personal commission to myself. For this I was born—that the world might know the love of God—because for this was Jesus born. For this I was born again. Jesus did not need to be, but I did. For this I was baptized, even as Jesus was baptized, as a part of His Messianic mission. We pastors certainly have no authority to baptize anyone who does not declare himself willing to take up the unfinished work of his Lord, any more than our government has the right to put a uniform on a soldier who does not dedicate himself to winning the war. For this I grew up, even as Jesus grew up to be the Savior of the world. It were better for your little child to die in infancy and go straight into the Lord's arms than to grow up and live a life of selfishness, utterly sundered from the great mission for which Christ came. For this I was educated. All the education in the world will be in the end but dust and ashes which has not had, as its great definite aim, the making known of the redemptive love and work of the Creator. For this I joined the Church. I did not see all of this then, but I see it now; for the Church is but the plant in the manufacturing sense, and the product or output of it must be the spread of the Gospel to all the world. Many look upon the Christian Church as a fine Pullman train to get them to heaven—a train made up of sleepers and diners and observation cars. The Christian Church is, indeed, a train; but it is such a train as I saw, when I was a boy pioneering upon the prairies of South Dakota—a train moving into the new country, a construction train to bring in the life and the power of the older civilization that we might conquer new areas.

No one has any business in the Christian Church who is not a worker, and therefore those churches are wise which declare in their constitutions that the church is a working body and has no place in it for those who will not work. If the church does not hear from a member either by contribution or attendance for two years, membership is automatically dropped. This makes it so that the worldly or worthless or spiritually indifferent son or daughter of deacon or trustee So-and-so can be put out of a hypocritical position, which his or her church membership is, without offense.

For the salvation of the world I am to have my pleasure, and for that alone. Jesus, as a youth, had His recreation; but you may be sure that nothing ever entered into it which was not refreshing to Him and which would not help Him forward in His great work. There are many pleasures that can be had in the right time to the glory of God. I have gone skating and fishing, because I was getting stale. But I have learned with joy never to indulge in sports where I do not take the Lord and where He does not counsel my going. One can play golf to the glory of God—not on the Sabbath, and not using the language that some people use. I know a vast number of young people and others who have found the glory of this principle; and once let this be admitted into the life of Christian young people, and the problem of pleasure is solved. "Whether ye eat or drink, or whatsoever you do, do all to the glory of God," says the Apostle Paul. We are proving in war time that everything can be done, even to rationing of food and to the cleaning up of our plates, for the winnnig of the war. Again he says (Col. 3: 17), "Whatsoever ye do in word or deed, do all in the name of the Lord Jesus Christ." "In the name of " means "representing," as with the power of attorney, representing as the traveling man represents the firm for which he travels. Let all Christians do this, and what would it mean for the lost ones of the world?

For this, the salvation of the world, I have a home, because it was for that reason that Jesus had a home. He came into an earthly home that the world might be saved. Before He was born, the thoughts and plans of Joseph and Mary centered about Him, and after His birth, throughout His earthly life, He was the center of that home. We have some homes that are missionary-minded. There was a young couple that planned to go out as missionaries, but were hindered, and they turned to farming in Kansas, determined that, if God gave them children, they would bring them up for the missionary work. As a result of this, six missionaries went forth. Why should not every home be thus centered in the salvation of the world? The Great Commission surrounds such a home, and everything done in it bears upon the spread of the Gospel.

For this, a Christian man has his business, because for the world's redemption the Lord, for many years, was a carpenter. That was a part of His redemptive work. There have been a few Christian businessmen who have said, " My business is serving the Lord, and I pack pork or do something else to pay expenses." All should have this principle. Preachers are no more called to advance the kingdom of our Lord than business and professional men are.

For this, the salvation of the world, I am to pray; because for this I shall be finally judged. There is coming a great judgment day, when the Lord will return, when His people shall be judged as to their work and shall receive awards or demerits in accordance with what they have done or failed to do, as we are plainly told in I Corinthians 3: 15, " If any man's work shall be burned, he shall suffer loss, yet he shall be saved, but so as by fire." The central question in that great event will be, " How has your life borne upon the evangelization and Christianization of the world? "

You may be absolutely sure that when our Lord went back to heaven, before He could sit down at the right hand of the Majesty on high, He had in some essential way to meet the Father's question, " Son, I sent you to the world to be its Savior. Did you do everything you possibly could do to make my love and my redemption known? " And we know very well that the Lord could not have sat down upon the throne of authority, nor would we be worshipping Him today, had He not been able to look the Father in the face and say, " Father, I did everything I possibly could do, moment by moment, to make Thy saving love known in the world."

Our eternal destiny, so far as our rewards affect it, is to be determined in heaven, to which we are brought by the redeeming grace of God, by the degree to which we can assert we have lived for that for which Jesus lived and died and rose again, and which He had committed to His Church to complete. We are saved by grace, but we are rewarded for our works. Paul shows us in the third chapter of first Corinthians that it is possible " to be saved yet suffering loss," like a man escaping from a burning building in his night clothes but losing all his possessions. This will be the fate of Christians who have not lived, as Christ lived, for the spread of the Gospel.

Let us reduce this to a helpful chart:

LIFE FOR THE CHRISTIAN

Matt. 28: 18–20, John 3: 17 and 20: 21
On the Authority of Christ
And in His Place

EVANGELIZE THE WORLD

For
This
{
I was born
I was born again
I grew up
I was baptized
I joined the church
I was educated
I have recreation
I have a home
I have a business
I pray and work
I will be judged

What About Missionary Work?

But the question will be asked, " Are we not promoting missions? " The answer must be, " Actually, yes; relatively, no." We are not promoting missions in proportion to the needs of the world. Far from it. With a billion and a half people outside of the Kingdom of the Son of God's love, we cannot say we are promoting missions. Converts in India number 300,000 a year, but the population increases by 5,000,000 a year!

We have not been promoting missions in proportion to opportunity. In China a thousand more missionaries, if not ten thousand, in the unoccupied regions would be greatly welcomed today. Before the war, doors were wide open everywhere, and millions were eagerly pressing for something better, and ready to listen to the Gospel. Additional thousands of missionaries are needed in India to cope with the opportunity which a population of nearly four hundred million presents. South America, for more than a generation, has been a vast and fertile missionary field. No, in reference to opportunity, the Christian Church has been doing comparatively nothing.

Neither have we been promoting missions in proportion to our ability. The Moravians, for many years, supported one missionary for every sixty of their members. The normal income in America today is around eighty billion dollars and constantly rising. Babson says that Christian people have more than one-half of this income. Let us suppose that they have one-half. A tithe of that would be four billion. Think of what that could mean for the Christianization of the world. For a number of years the evangelical churches of America have contributed for the work outside of America $30,000,000 per year, an average of about a dollar a piece per member for 365 days—a cent every three days. Last year there was spent in America for patented dog food alone $60,000,000. Four hundred and fifty million dollars for cosmetics, two billion dollars burned up into tobacco smoke, three billion dollars spent for alcoholic beverages, three billion dollars gambled away, fifteen billion dollars spent for the arrest and trial and punishment of criminals—to give only a few annual expenditures! How insignificant mission and Church figures look in comparison with these other expenditures! The President asked for one lump of $56,000,000,000 in one year, and he got it. It would take the Church, spending thirty million dollars a year for missions, 1866 years to use fifty-six billion dollars. The

Laymen's Missionary Movement, a number of years ago, figured out if we could get an average of ten cents per week per member from all of the members of our evangelical churches for foreign missions, amounting to $5.20 a year, we could give to every 25,000 of the world's unevangelized population not only a preaching station, but a school and a hospital. Anyone would know that within a generation each 25,000 could in some measure be evangelized. Therefore, the slogan of the Student Volunteer Movement a generation ago, "The Evangelization of the World in This Generation," was not simply religious enthusiasm; it was what could have been done without even anything approaching sacrifice. Ten cents per week per member! How the dimes slip away for nonessentials! How pitiable the sum seems in reference to the world's need! Three stamps and a postal card per week! Two packages of gum! The comparisons would be ridiculous if they were not so devastatingly true. A dime seems insignificant today, except when men come to church. Then it seems as large as a wagon wheel!

We have not promoted missions as we shall wish we had when the Son of man comes to reckon with His Church. The government points a finger of scorn at the Christian Church in allowing a deduction of fifteen per cent of income as non-taxable, while the amount deducted is, on the average, only about two per cent. All of the money spent for all local expenses of the church, for all the work at home, in our buildings and in their maintenance, amounts to but three per cent of the Christian's income, while that contributed to missions is but one-third of one per cent instead of the seven per cent which the Lord should have for saving the lost in the world. How will this pittance look when we stand before the Lord who gave His *all?* I have just received a letter from a pastor stating that last year his church, though it has a current expense budget of $6,000, gave

$14,000 to missions. This, the normal, is the rarest of exceptions.

The Threefold Way of Promotion

There are three ways in which we can promote missions. First, by prayer—prayer for the laborers who are in the field, prayer for more harvest hands, prayer for the overthrow of heathenism. A missionary in southern China told me that he was convinced that if we could have a campaign of prayer for the missionary work similar to that which we have for money and for men, we would see heathenism crumble before our very eyes; yet there are few Christians who pray regularly for the missionary work.

The second way to promote missions is by personal consecration to the task, the willingness to go forth in the name of our Lord. Not all people can do that, but many must; and many more would go if we had more adequate support. There are literally thousands of young people today who would spring to the task if they knew that an aroused church was back of them.

The third way is to go by proxy. What you pay to missions measures your personality in that work. You are that much of a missionary. Look at yourself in your contribution. You are witnessing that much.

If we were to carry out the principle of tithing taught in the Old Testament, one-tenth of our income would go directly to the support of Christian leaders. Therefore, we could have one in the service actually preaching the Gospel somewhere in the world for every ten heads of family at least. And, as the Israelites gave a second tithe for their sacrifices, we could support our local church on that second tithe, and then look after all of the other social needs with the tithe every third year, or the one-third of a tithe, that the devoted

Jews gave from the time of Ezra to the time of Christ. How much of a missionary are you?

We must face the bitter fact that because we would not give our money for spreading the Gospel, we are now having to pay it out for guns. That which we would not spend for missions we must now spend for munitions. That which we would not give in tithes we have now to give, and much more, in taxes. We are having to pay for bombers because we did not, when we had the opportunity, flood the world with Bibles. No man who has complained that his church gives too much for missions has any just ground for complaint if his son is sacrificed in a war that is upon us because of the inadequacy of our missionary enterprise.

What Is Your Response?

What is your answer to all of these facts—that the Church was launched with a purpose, program, and power sufficient to have changed world conditions steadily for the better; that the good and the blessing, the joy and the peace which have been in the world are the fruits of the Gospel which even a perverted Church has given to the world; that the evils which are dominant in the world and this present awful war are but the penalty of the Church's perversions, paralysis, and pernicious practices; that we can still have, if we will, for God wills it, a Church of mighty regenerating, reforming, cleansing, Christianizing power at work in the world?

" If my people, which are called by my name, shall humble themselves, and pray, and seek my face, and turn from their wicked ways; then will I hear from heaven, and will forgive their sin, and will heal their land " (II Chron. 7: 14).

Let us hear the call of Bishop A. R. Coxe:

" We are living, we are dwelling
In a grand and awful time;

In an age, on ages telling,
To be living is sublime.

" Hark! The waking up of nations,
God and Magog to the fray;
Hark! What soundeth is creation
Groaning for its latter day.

" Will ye play, then? Will ye dally
With your music and your wine?
Up! It is JEHOVAH'S RALLY!
God's own arm hath need of thine.

" Hark! the onset; will ye fold your
Faith-clad arms in lazy lock?
Up, oh, up, thou drowsy soldier!
Worlds are charging to the shock!

" Fear not, spurn the worldling's laughter;
Thine ambition—trample thou!
Thou shalt find a *long* HEREAFTER,
TO BE MORE than tempts thee now.

" On! LET ALL YOUR SOUL WITHIN YOU
For the truth's sake go abroad!
Strike!   Let every nerve and sinew
TELL ON AGES . . . TELL FOR GOD! "